An Actor's Tricks

by Yoshi Oida and Lorna Marshall
An Actor Adrift
The Invisible Actor

by Lorna Marshall
The Body Speaks

AN
ACTOR'S
TRICKS

Yoshi Oida and Lorna Marshall

Methuen Drama

Published by Methuen Drama

1 3 5 7 9 10 8 6 4 2

First published 2007
Methuen Drama
A & C Black Publishers Limited
38 Soho Square
London W1D 3HB
www.acblack.com

A CIP catalogue record for this book is available from the British Library

ISBN 978 0 413 77449 1

Typeset in 10pt Janson Text by SX Composing DTP, Rayleigh, Essex
Printed and bound in Great Britain by Bookmarque Ltd, Croydon, Surrey

Contents

Foreword

The proof of the pudding

In the East, a teacher never teaches. At least, not in the way we think. A true teacher never explains, never gives out recipes. He – or sometimes she – is a living example of what is possible, of what can be achieved with endless patience and unshakeable determination.

One of our musicians went to India to learn to play a very special form of horn unknown in the West. After a long search he found a teacher. The teacher never spoke, he simply played. First simple notes, then a few notes together and occasionally a complex series of magnificent sounds. Day after day, the pupil was encouraged to do the same. For many weeks he blew, cheeks swollen, muscles tense but no sound came. Then, suddenly one day, an ugly snort burst out of the instrument. It was a beginning and now he listened to the teacher more deeply, trying to understand, passing through moments of utter despair. At last the day came when quite naturally he found he could play. The instrument was no stranger, it had become his own.

However, nothing in the Oriental tradition can be applied directly to the West. This is what first brought Yoshi Oida to Europe. What lessons could he find in this unknown hemisphere? In his books, he generously shares with us his search. He reveals his difficulties and vividly evokes the examples past and present that have guided him over the years. He refrains from giving out methods and he does not try to teach. Instead, with humour and modesty he brings his working day to life – with its dreams, its defeats, its ideals and its discoveries – nourished by the special understanding given to him by his own tradition.

But he tricks us with his title. There are no tricks, there are no explanations. There are only experiences. This is the real teaching.

Peter Brook
Paris, 16 November 2006

Introduction

People often ask how our books (this one as well as *The Invisible Actor*) have been put together. Over the years, Yoshi and I have spent many hours discussing theatre and various aspects of Japanese practice and culture. Out of those conversations I wrote the bulk of the text, using Yoshi's ideas and typical voice. I then added other sections in my own voice, usually to clarify a point or to add background on some aspect of Japanese culture. My interpolations are in *italics*, followed by *L.M.*

In addition I have written an appendix on training (and the problems involved in describing what is essentially a living, dynamic process). This is my own point of view, but since Yoshi and I have worked together extensively (on taught workshops and theatrical productions, as well as three books), his influence is inevitably present. The exercises I outline are ones I have observed him teach in workshops; nevertheless, the descriptions and interpretations (and any errors) are my own.

As both of us are aware, creative process is elusive and individual. There are no fixed techniques, or recipes to be followed that guarantee success. What works for one person will be irrelevant to another. And much will depend on when and where a person encounters an idea or experience. This problem is even greater when it comes to writing down artistic concepts and processes in concrete phrases. One particular idea might open an entire universe of possibility to one reader, seem trite and obvious to a second, and totally incomprehensible to a third. For this reason there are no prescriptions in this book, only our personal interests and experiences, plus some suggestions and hints. We hope they may prove useful.

I would like to thank the Arts and Humanities Research Council of Great Britain, and the Daiwa Anglo-Japanese Foundation, whose generous fellowship gave me the time to write this book.

Lorna Marshall

'A certain actor had a son who was twelve or thirteen years old and was attending school. He said to him, "Things which an actor need not learn are the use of the abacus, and calligraphy, and there are also several other things that he can ignore." Tojuro [a famous Kabuki actor] heard this and said, "No, no, that is not true at all. The actor's art is like the beggar's bag. Regardless of whether you need it at the time or not, you should pick up everything as you come across it and take it away with you. You should make use only of those things which you need, and those you do not you should put on one side and bring out when you need them. There must not be anything about which you are entirely ignorant. Even purse-cutting [pick-pocketing] should be carefully studied." '

The Actor's Analects; Dust in the Ears, Item XIX (translator: Charles J. Dunn, Columbia University Press, New York, 1969)

1 The Morning of the Show

It's morning. Light seeps into my bedroom and I start to wake up. As my mind begins surfacing, I remember that today is a performance day. Tonight I will be on the stage.

I have to be ready to work, so the first thing I do is to check through my body. Is it available? Yes, basically it is fine; no pain, no aches.

I sit up in my bed, and now I become aware that my lower back is tight and uncomfortable. Not unusual at my age, but not helpful either. So I know I need to stretch. I get out of my bed and stretch through the whole body; spine, legs, arms and shoulders, everywhere. This takes around twenty minutes. Now my body is easier and more alive.

Once my joints and muscles start to loosen, I begin checking inside my body. Not to see how my intestines are functioning, but something quite different.

We are all aware of our physical structure, but what makes this collection of bones and muscles move? Maybe everything comes from the brain, I don't know. Whatever its point of origin, it does seem as if human beings have some kind of inner energy. Like a huge fire inside our body. But usually that energy is hidden and people cannot see it from the outside. In a way, our bodies are like the earth itself. The outside of our planet is normally very quiet and unchanging to our eyes, but if you observe an erupting volcano, you can suddenly see fire breaking through the earth's crust. This fire actually fills the whole interior of the planet and its edge lies just a short distance under the surface. It is always there, but unless we are near a volcano we don't see it.

In performance, if the actor can find a way to contact the fire that exists inside the body, the audience can share that energy. We need to be like a volcano, able to let our energy erupt into the world. This inner fire is related to the presence of the actor. We all know that when certain actors stand still, or simply walk on to the stage, you feel some kind of presence; you want to watch them. Other actors seem to be very far away and you aren't interested in what they do or say. But why aren't all actors equally fascinating to watch?

There isn't a clear answer to this question, but I have noticed that in many cases there seem to be complexes and blocks coming from the actors' intellectual control, and also from their emotions (both positive or negative). These prevent the energy coming out. So the next question is: how do you get rid of these intellectual or emotional barriers?

Through my experience of watching and directing performers (singers as well as actors), I discovered a pattern. I found that people who do regular bodywork somehow have a stronger presence on stage. So perhaps one way to unblock the inner energy is to work regularly with the body. In this way the energy can become more available to the actor and visible to the audience. But this raises a further question: what kind of work? Stretching seems to be a good thing to do (and I know I should stretch my body even on days when I don't have a show). For this reason many actors follow a formal stretching programme, or use specific physical exercises to prepare the body on a daily basis.

However, there is one factor to consider. Sometimes exercises which link stretching to relaxation can make you become soft and sleepy, or just give you a pleasant physical sensation. The same thing can happen when you do pure breath work. While it is necessary to stretch the body, becoming soft and sleepy is no use for the actual performance. In the same way normal physical exercises (like going to the gym, or a dance class) are not what you want in theatre. They use a lot of body effort and leave you with a feeling of comfortable, agreeable tiredness. This is also not for the theatre. You must choose your system carefully, or adapt what you learn in order to be truly alive on stage.

So how do we work with the body in such a way as to make our fire stronger and more available? People often ask me which particular technique I would recommend as regular training, but in fact there are a number of systems that can be useful; you must find the one that works best for you, or develop your own.

In the previous book, *The Invisible Actor*, I talked about certain areas of the body and their importance for the job of acting. While I don't want to repeat things too much, there are some additional points that might be useful.

ANUS

When we look at a dog, his tail is a good indicator of how he is feeling. Fear makes his coccyx tuck under until the tail is hidden between his legs, but when he is excited the coccyx moves out in order to lift the tail into the air. Unhappy, the tail goes under. Happy or ready to fight, the tail goes up. Human beings also have a tail, right at the end of the spine near the anus. As people get older, they gradually lose their energy and their tail (or coccyx) may tend to tuck under. If we look at an old man or woman, we can often see that the coccyx is tucked right underneath a bent spine. Since it isn't angled out enough, back pain and stiffness can result.

To enhance our basic energy on the stage, it is nice to keep the coccyx very slightly out. Like a bird. Of course, you cannot actually lift the coccyx free of the body, like a dog's tail, but you can give a tiny outward tilt at the very base of the spine. This is the form used in the Noh Theatre.

There are three major styles of classical theatre in Japan: Noh Theatre, Kabuki and Bunraku, all created before the eighteenth century. These styles are still performed today in something close to their original form and have a devoted audience following. In all three styles the traditions are handed down and maintained by specific families and only male actors are permitted to perform on the professional stage, although non-family members can take classes as amateurs.

As a young man, Yoshi received training within these traditions. Since he often refers to concepts and techniques from these sources, some background information might be useful. In particular, he often draws on his training in the Noh Theatre.

Noh Theatre came into existence at the beginning of the fourteenth century and was codified by its great Master, Motokiyo Zeami. It is a minimalist theatre, using an empty stage, no set and only a few props to suggest whatever reality is being evoked. On the other hand the costumes are gorgeous. It has two distinct sub-forms: Noh and Kyogen. The first form, Noh, is a highly stylised masked theatre, with ritualistic dance movements, musical accompaniment (drums and flute), a chorus and heightened use of the voice on the part of the actors. Its themes tend to be melancholy, concerned with longing, loss, and the uncertainty of life and love. The various stories are arranged into five categories: Gods, Warriors, Unfortunate Women, Madwomen and Demons. Despite the extremity of the characters there is very little expressed emotion, or direct conflict, and few spectacular effects.

The second form in Noh Theatre is Kyogen, which is a broad comic style involving elements of farce. The stories are down to earth, with tales of stupid gods, ugly wives, and (very typically) a master and two cunning servants. In Kyogen the language is more naturalistic, as is the acting style.

Noh and Kyogen were traditionally performed alongside each other in a single programme, with five Noh plays and four Kyogen being staged in alternance. In this way the audience was moved from tragedy to comedy to tragedy and so on through the nine plays. Although this extended programme is performed less frequently today, it is important to understand that the two styles were traditionally seen as totally complementary.

Similar technical skills, such as ways of moving and singing, are shared between the two forms and both involve stylisation (although this is more visibly evident in Noh than it is in Kyogen). However, despite sharing a stage and a tradition, there is no overlap between the training and repertoire of the actors themselves. While there is occasionally a Kyogen character in a Noh play, only Noh actors perform the main roles in Noh plays, and only Kyogen actors perform Kyogen plays. But it is the combination of Noh and Kyogen that constitutes the Noh Theatre. L.M.

In the Noh Theatre there are specific techniques for singing. One of these employs a focus on the very base of the spine. When you go up in pitch, you tighten the anus. In addition, you imagine the voice travels up the spinal column as the pitch goes higher. And when you go down in pitch, you imagine that the sound moves down the front of the body, right down into the belly. In Noh, rising sounds go up the back, descending sounds travel down the front. This is similar to certain ideas in yoga practice.

In general, when an actor is shouting or angry or moving strongly, it is a good idea to tighten the anus. Try doing a strong action in the normal way, then do it again while clenching the anus. See if there is a difference. When you tighten the anus you might feel a kind of shock to the top of the head. In fact, the two ends of the spine seem to be related and our energy passes between these two points. In addition, when you shout on stage the neck often becomes tight and the voice becomes strangled. But if you think very strongly about tightening the anus when you make a loud sound, the throat remains relaxed and there is less risk of damaging your voice.

THE *HARA*

In the classical Japanese theatre, people constantly refer to *hara*. You are taught to move from the *hara*, you try to catch the *hara* of the character and you face your partner with *hara*. Actors laugh from the *hara*, scream in rage from the *hara*, cry from the *hara*. Without an internal connection to the *hara*, the outside cannot function properly for an actor. So before actors do an outward action, they must connect with the *hara* and proceed from there.

Unfortunately, nobody can define exactly what the *hara* is, not even the Japanese. Literally it means 'belly', both outside and inside, and refers to the area located between the navel and the top of the pubic bone. But the function of the *hara* transcends a simple anatomical location.

In the Noh Theatre my teachers always stressed the importance of maintaining energy in the *hara* and to be aware of it in all of my actions. I learned that when Noh actors walk, it is the *hara* that travels forwards and the body follows. In the same way when they turn to walk in another direction, they don't just turn their feet. Instead, the *hara* changes direction first and the feet respond. When they kneel, the *hara* descends. When they rise, the *hara* lifts and continues moving upwards, bringing the rest of the body with it. All actions begin in the *hara* and the body follows. Moving from the *hara* makes the movements appear organic.

I have already mentioned tightening the anus when you need to produce a loud sound, such as screaming or shouting. In the same way you can also focus on the *hara* when you need to use a strong vocal energy, especially one linked to an emotional or dramatic climax. In fact, any emotional state should go down to the *hara*. When you are in an emotional state you will, of course, feel it in the chest, but you should try to also connect it downwards to the *hara*, rather than letting it escape upwards into yelling, arm waving and too much demonstration.

In real life, when you meet somebody important, or someone you respect, or you find yourself in a difficult situation mentally or emotionally, or you are afraid or angry, your body responds. And one thing that commonly occurs is that your shoulders go up. On stage, because you are usually scared or excited, the same thing happens: your body changes and your shoulders go up. But as a performer you have to be careful to bring the shoulders down. If they stay up you look frightened and you can damage your voice. Of course, sometimes the shoulders need to be up if this is right for the character, but basically try to keep them down. Don't worry about trying to change your feelings, or telling yourself 'Relax. Relax.' Just bring the shoulders down. Focusing on the shoulders is better than saying 'relax', since 'relax' doesn't usually produce good acting. As I said earlier, actors don't want to be 'relaxed'; they want to be free and alive. Connecting to your point when feeling strong emotions is another way to prevent the shoulder rising upwards.

Of course, if you try to follow all these instructions at the same time it is impossible. You can't do anything. When you perform on the stage, you forget all these instructions. But they are useful to explore when you are practising or training.

THE STERNUM

For the actor, the sternum is also important, since emotional activity is linked to that area of the body. For example, when people change emotions from happy to sad, the placement of the sternum usually alters. When we are hopeful the sternum tends to go forward and up: it lifts. And when we are sad, the sternum tends to sink down and back, collapsing the chest inwards. The actual movements might not be very big, but the connection between the sternum and our inner life is clear.

We can apply this connection in the opposite direction to help us perform. When rehearsing, or exploring emotions, try secretly lifting the sternum upwards, or dropping it downwards, or shifting it forwards or backwards. See if this changes the internal state of your emotions. Try many different positions for the sternum (shifted backwards but with a slight upwards tilt, or strongly pushed forward and so on) and see what emotions these positions might connect to. In addition, playing with the various positions allows you to practise keeping the sternum alive. When you perform you are not aware of your sternum, but if it is free and used to being alive, the public can see your emotional state. The sternum draws emotions from you and at the same time shows your emotions to the audience.

However, the shoulders and the sternum are not a single unit; the sternum is capable of moving independently of the shoulders. Too often actors fix sternum and shoulders into a single rigid triangle in an attempt to improve their posture, so that when they move the chest, the entire upper body follows. In fact, you need a fluid sternum; one that can shift in any direction without necessarily engaging the shoulders. If your sternum is rigid, you can look tight and armoured on stage, and your emotional responses may be impeded. A fluid sternum helps you to look alive and to respond naturally. These independent movements of the sternum can be quite subtle; they don't need to be big to be effective.

In African dance, the sternum is taught to make circles in the vertical direction. The shoulders don't move in space (they are a fixed point), but the chest goes up, forward, down, back and so on round. Then you do the circle in the reverse direction as well. This helps to loosen the sternum and allows it to respond. When doing this work, it is also interesting to look for the relationship between the sternum and the tailbone. For example, when your sternum makes the circle, the tailbone can move in and out. Working like this increases the flexibility and responsiveness in the entire torso. In addition, because the nerves connecting the body to the brain pass down the body via the interior of the spinal column, moving the spine seems to provide the nerves with stimulation, like a massage. So they become more sensitive.

THE CENTRE LINE OF THE BODY

A Japanese philosopher made a request of his student. He suggested that whenever the student read a book, or listened to a teacher, he should maintain good posture – good posture and calm breathing. Traditionally, most teachers in Japan make this demand, since it seems that you learn more effectively when your body is aligned. Your comprehension of what the teacher is saying or the book is saying is better.

But posture doesn't mean being stiff. You should be straight, but also relaxed. The Japanese word 'judo' is made up of two concepts; the '*ju*' means 'soft/gentle' and '*do*' is 'the way'. So the whole word means 'the way of softness'. When you are soft you can move the body easily, and your energy can develop and expand.

We are all aware of the line of our spine as it runs down the back of our bodies, but there is another line that runs through your body: the centre line. This runs from the forehead to the groove under the nose, to the throat, to the sternum, to the navel, to the *hara* and finally it turns underneath to join the anus. This line is on the outside of the body until the throat, then it continues downwards inside the body, like a skewer through a kebab. However, skewers are rigid, while this line is soft and flexible, like rubber.

Awareness of this centre line can also give you a different sense of your body. In particular, it makes you more aware of the two halves of your body – the right side and the left side – and how this body connects to the wider space around it.

Yoshi trained for a number of years in Kyogen and often refers to the advice of his Kyogen teacher. As mentioned earlier, both Noh and Kyogen styles are maintained by a number of families, who pass on the specific techniques and traditions to the following generations. The head of each family is responsible for managing the performing company, organising the repertoire and maintaining the techniques and training. In Noh there are five acting dynasties, in Kyogen there are currently only two families.

Yoshi's teacher Yataro Okura was the head of the Okura tradition of Kyogen. L.M.

My teacher, Master Okura, used to tell me that when you are dealing with matters involving the right side of the stage, use the right side of your body, i.e. the right leg and arm. When you deal with things involving the left side of the stage, use the left side of the body. Don't cross the centre line of the body. For example, if you point to somebody who is standing on the right side of your body, you use the right hand. Someone on your left is indicated by the left hand. In addition, if the choreography requires you to indicate a broad sweep of space with one hand only, you still avoid crossing the centre line of the body. For example, if you use the right hand to indicate a direction from stage right to stage left. You begin by facing the audience and move the right hand from out from the right side, then start sweeping it towards the left. Once the hand reaches centre stage on its arc, you swivel the whole body to the left in order to continue the action. The hand itself doesn't travel across the centre line of the body.

As an exercise, to help you understand the harmony of your body, keep an awareness of this centre line and move the body symmetrically. In daily life we never move symmetrically. We tend to do things with one hand or one leg at a time. We even lean or slump our torsos in an asymmetric position when we are sitting. You can do any kind of movement with the arms, legs, shoulders, elbows, feet and so on, even your fingers. Improvise and try to find out all of the possibilities of the body while remaining completely symmetrical. Walking is the exception, since otherwise you can only jump in order to displace the body using both legs symmetrically. So feel free to walk around the space, while keeping the rest of your actions symmetrical. And you should keep the head free, since you need to stay aware of what is happening around you.

OTHER KINDS OF DAILY PREPARATION

Ki

In 1973 I went with Peter's group on a wonderful journey through Africa. We travelled from Algeria, through the Sahara desert to Nigeria and Benin (and back again), performing in various villages along the way. When doing these performances we would place a carpet on the ground, then improvise from zero. Somebody would start some kind of story and we all would try to develop this into a performance lasting about forty-five minutes. One thing I remember from this time was one of the other actors asking me about the somersault I had done when performing. I was surprised and said, 'But I cannot do somersaults!' He replied that I had definitely performed a somersault on the carpet. I truly could not remember doing it, but it happened all the same. In a way, the pressure of improvisation and the panic about creating a show led me to do something which I didn't know I could do. I must have had the ability to do a somersault, but in normal performances I stayed within the territory I knew, using my ordinary range and power.

It seems that we have more possibilities as actors than we realise. Usually, when we perform, we stay within our normal consciousness and understanding. We do what we know we can do. Yet when we find ourselves in a state of panic or confusion a power we are unaware of sometimes emerges. There is something deeper. Being too focused on your conscious intelligence and analytical skills can limit you; you have to become aware that there are other possibilities hidden within. Without this broader awareness, you cannot get power beyond the normal state of daily existence. You cannot evoke that kind of energy.

But once you are aware of this power, how do you evoke it?

In Japanese this subtle energy is called *ki*, but since there is no equivalent word in European languages, it is very difficult to explain. You cannot see or touch *ki*. It isn't inside the five senses. You can feel it, if you are sufficiently sensitive, but most people aren't aware of it. It is something hidden behind the material reality. When you open the branch of the tree, you cannot find the baby flower. But there is some invisible life force or energy in the tree that makes a flower. It cannot be explained scientifically at this present time, but maybe in a few years scientists will clarify the existence of *ki* and how it operates.

According to the Eastern system of acupuncture, the body is seen as containing lines of energy, which connect various organs and physical functions. These meridians are a materialised expression of *ki*. The operation of chemistry in the body is also linked to *ki*. Although *ki* is not a part of your mind, you can use your mind to evoke the function of *ki*, then the body can act with *ki*.

Aikido might be a good general starting point to look at how *ki* could be developed, since the literal translation of the word is 'the way (*do*) of the meeting/exchange (*ai*) of *ki*'.

In fact, all the traditional martial arts of Japan acknowledge the importance of *ki*; they know fighting involves something more than muscles. If you can fight with *ki*, your combat is stronger than anything you can achieve through muscle strength. Champion fighters are always looking for ways to enhance and channel their *ki*, even in what appears to be an ordinary situation.

There is another possible path to explore. In the late twentieth century, Haruchika Noguchi (who was originally a traditional masseur) created a method of self-massage and healing called *seitai*. He said that modern people are very developed in terms of intelligence, but they need to go back to a more primitive state of the body, since they have lost contact with our source of deep energy. He suggested many exercises, including one called *yukiho* (*yu* is the 'path through/to', *ki* is energy, *ho* is 'method'). Through your mind you can either bring *ki* together and hold it, or you send it away. You combine breathing and your imagination with the physical exercise.

In fact, from what I have observed, *ki* relates to three elements: breathing, spine and imagination.

Actors already know the importance of developing their breathing and there are many good systems for working on this area. Try studying with different teachers until you find an approach that suits you. But awareness of breath is not confined to working with the lungs. For example, in all forms of traditional Japanese martial arts training, when you enter the exercise space you bow. And before the tournament you bow to the other people. Not for religious reasons. It also isn't a simple question of formality. When you bow it is related to your breathing. Normally, when you bow, you breathe out. This is the physical pattern. And as you breathe out, your energy goes to your partner. This helps you to develop your breathing and, with your partner, you can exchange energy. Bowing also helps you to connect to the centre line of the body. In addition, when you bow with your partner, you can feel the spatial relationship between the two of you. Plus you calm yourself down and, because of this calm, you can move freely. In fact, a simple action can contain many possibilities.

I have already talked a lot about the second element of *ki* (the spine) both here and in *The Invisible Actor*. The third element, imagination, is also interesting for the actor.

You can try something yourself. Stand in a clear space with one person on either side of you. Bend your arms at right angles, but keep your upper arms close to the body, so that your lower arms protrude forward at a horizontal angle, parallel to the floor. Your partners grip your elbows and wrists from underneath. They then attempt to lift you straight up, off the floor.

For the first round, imagine that you are already flying up towards the sky while your partners attempt to lift you. Then repeat the exercise imagining that you are going down into the earth. You don't change what your body is doing, only your imagination. Yet somehow the weight of your body feels different. Usually the lifters also experience a clear difference between the two actions; in the first version they normally manage to get a definite degree of lift (the height depends on how light the person is and how strong the lifters are), while in the second case there is often a struggle to get any upward movement at all. For the other people your imagination has somehow changed the weight of your body. Of course, the actual physical weight of the body remains unchanged; you haven't suddenly lost ten kilos. Perhaps it is a case of the imagination altering our energy and that different energy affecting the physical relationship with other people

There seem to be a variety of ways to connect to *ki*. All children like to hug big trees and somehow to make contact with them. So do I. This isn't just a matter of skin meeting bark, but of something deep, from my *hara*, connecting to the deep life energy of the tree. Unfortunately, when I do this in a public park I get very strange looks. It is better to find a nice private forest.

I once heard that during the Second World War some Dutch prisoners found a way to help themselves when they got sick. There were no medicines, no doctors or nurses, but they discovered that holding a patient close in their arms made a difference. The position of the two bodies was important; the patient faced the helper, making sure that the entire torsos were in contact with each other. This position was maintained for extended periods. They also focused on feelings of love and affection while they were embracing. In this way both the body and the feeling of the helpers came together. And somehow this treatment worked. Outside sexual activity, our relations with other people are rarely physical. We may talk and laugh together, or walk alongside each other, but we seldom connect with other people's bodies. The body itself, however, is not just skin and muscle and bone, it is something else as well.

A master chef of sushi once said that if you make the rice patties for sushi with a machine it tastes less good. You must make the patties by hand. If sushi is made by hand, the *ki* of the chef exits the body via the palm and goes into the rice, and this makes it taste better.

Purification

Every morning, you brush your teeth and you wash your body, but what about your spirit? Most of us believe we have both body and spirit, but in the rush of daily life it is easy to forget about the second part. You know your body must be clean and fresh, but your spirit needs to be cleaned up as well. This is something that is good to do every day (like brushing your teeth), but it is especially important when you are preparing for a performance.

The ancient Shinto religion of Japan places great emphasis on purification, in terms of both theology and practice. According to the Shinto creation story, the god Izanagi descended into the underworld of the dead. On his return, he bathed to purify his body, and as he cleansed himself other gods, entities and land masses came into being. In this way creation and purification are directly linked. Followers of Shinto will wash their bodies every morning by bathing in cold water (ideally in the sea or a mountain waterfall, but a cold shower in the bathroom is also considered effective). In addition, meditation is used to cleanse the spirit of the impurities created through the pressures of daily life. L.M.

In traditional Japanese calligraphy, a brush is used to place black lines of liquid ink onto a white sheet of paper. Then meaning appears. White paper on its own doesn't communicate anything. Only when the black marks are present can meaning appear. The white has meaning because of the black. Equally, if the white isn't present, the black cannot create meaning.

But if the paper is already dirty the meaning cannot come out. Too much grime and dirt makes the brush strokes hard to read. It is the same when you act. It isn't enough just to be your ordinary daily self; you have to purify your existence, so that what you are communicating can be clearly understood.

When I look at my life since I was born, I can see that my white paper has become quite dirty. There is a lot of grime in my life.

People say, 'This is my character, or my life experience.' You can take this in a positive way, but you can equally view it negatively. Because of my knowledge and experience my paper has become marked and grubby, and it is harder for the brush strokes to be read. And much of my experience has no special quality; it is simply habit. But at least I can try to clean up my paper, so that what is written on it is as clear as possible to the audience.

So how can we clean it up? There is no single system. Some people do meditation, according to various traditions, or chant, or do deep breathing. Others might engage in the tea ceremony, or work in their garden, or have cold-water showers, or go walking in the forest, or listen to music, or hug other people.

It is interesting that a number of these purification practices once again involve the spine. In meditation and some forms of chanting the spine is held in a straight line, while in certain exercises from *aikido* the spine moves in either a figure of eight or a spiral. In Africa, before going hunting, the men do a dance, which is a preparatory ritual for the chase. In this dance the spine moves in a wavelike form. In fact, African dance uses a lot of movements that involve action of the spine; undulations of the spine from the tailbone to the top of the skull, plus circling movements of the sternum. We know these are good for the body, but maybe this also helps cleanse the spirit. I don't know. There are many possibilities, but whatever you prefer, I feel it is necessary to purify the spirit. Each person has his or her own way or method.

According to Shinto belief, when you are born you are completely pure, like a god. Then, as you go through life, you get a lot of 'dust' on your being, both physical and spiritual. For this reason the essence of Shinto practice is purification, to return to the state in which you were born. There are similar beliefs in other religions. According to esoteric Buddhism, when you are born the first thing you do is make the sound 'Ah'. Which is the sound of pure creation. In this tradition the practitioners spend their whole lives trying to rediscover that first effortless sound 'Ah'.

2 On the Way to the Theatre

On the way to the theatre I often stop in a café. As I drink my coffee I enjoy watching the people go by. People sit in cafés for many reasons; some admire the architecture of the historical street, or they enjoy the warm air, or the music in the background, or the clothes and fashion that are on display. But I am only interested in watching how people behave, out there on the street. But not only the life of human beings; even animals are interesting to watch. A dog waiting for his master outside a shop, what is his life while he is waiting? What is happening in the brain? What is happening inside? This is fascinating.

It is the same for me in the theatre. If I see beautiful costumes or set or lighting, it is nice, but five minutes later I get bored. But when the people move I never get bored. Human life is the most interesting thing to see in the theatre – human beings and what is happening inside them. It doesn't matter if it is stylised, like Japanese classical theatre, or opera, or dance; or realistic theatre, like Chekhov. What is important is that through the movement, through the voice, through the music, through the dance, I begin to sense how the human being lives.

But what you see in the theatre isn't the same as what you see on the street. Theatre selects, and compresses, and distils real life. It is never a straight documentary. Chekhov might appear more 'realistic' than Beckett, but neither Chekhov nor Beckett simply takes a slice of life and puts it on the stage. For example, the timescale of the performance isn't realistic; five minutes on the stage might represent five years in the lives of the individuals. As an actor playing in these pieces, the solution is not to attempt to imitate the surface of life directly. Instead, we need to understand what lies behind each moment of real life. And how that links to interactions in the world. And this is the aim of the rehearsal process: to find this life. But how?

ARTIST'S INTELLIGENCE

Peter Brook once told me a story about the great painter Cézanne. When he painted still lifes, he placed the pots, the flowers, the knife and so on perfectly, in front of him ready to be painted. But somehow he was not fully satisfied with this composition, so he decided to walked round the arrangement, looking at it from different angles. Suddenly, when he was behind the composition he stopped, recognising that this new angle was much more interesting to paint. And this is what he did. His initial step was to arrange his subject perfectly via his own intellect and aesthetic sense, and for many people this would have been enough, but Cézanne wasn't satisfied. Something more was needed.

A good artist doesn't only follow his own logical intelligence; instead, he understands that being open to other ways of discovery is also necessary.

During the production of *Qui est là* at the Bouffes du Nord (1995), I spoke a text from Stanislavky:

J'arrange les meubles, les chaises. Je place les acteurs. Il faut être comme dans la vie. La scène c'est un miroir de la vie. Il faut être vrai. J'ai conçu très soigneusement mes mises en scène pour que tout soit vrai. Mais le résultat ne reflet pas la vérité; c'est un miroir de mes idées. Que faire? Je me mets de côté, derrière, de l'autre côte. Mais je vois tout, j'entends tout, je comprends tout. C'est beaucoup plus vivant.

[I arrange the furnishings, the chairs. I place the actors. It must be as it is in real life. The stage is a mirror of life. It must be true. I have very carefully considered my directing approach so that everything is true. But the result does not reflect reality; it is a mirror of my ideas. What can I do? I place myself to one side [of the stage], then I go behind, then to the other side. But I see everything, I hear everything, I understand everything. It is much more alive.]

Stanislavsky placed everything perfectly to reflect real life. But in the end he didn't remain with that version. Like Cézanne, he wasn't satisfied with the initial idea, since he realised that this was only the product of his intellect. So then he walked 360 degrees round the whole set, looking for the best position for the audience's eye. By going round the furniture he discovered a better arrangement and shifted the set accordingly. He wasn't content with his own intelligence, or the initial conscious artistic decision. Maybe we can think about acting in the same way.

As an actor during rehearsal, you use your conscious intelligence and insight to research the background and world of the play. You read books or gather information by talking to people. In addition, you work on the text to ensure that you understand exactly what you are saying. You analyse meaning and search for a psychological understanding of the situations and characters. All this is essential to produce work that is accurate and detailed. But too often the actor's work ends there; we think this is more than enough to ensure a good performance.

And on one level it is true; this kind of work will produce a good, correct performance. But is this why the audience comes to the theatre? Only to see an accurate, logical, clearly articulated interpretation?

I feel that audiences want something more, something beyond the logical and the everyday. Something that stirs them on a deeper level. And for this I feel actors need another, additional kind of intelligence.

At the beginning of the twentieth century Taisetsu Suzuki developed various concepts from Zen Buddhism for a Western audience. In his book *Zen Buddhism and Its Influence on Japanese Culture* he noted that there were three kinds of knowledge.

The first kind of knowledge comes via reading or hearing. We remember this type of information and carry it with us as a possession. For example, if you want to understand the earth, you cannot do it directly; you cannot walk over the entire planet. You must read a map created by other people, then you put this understanding into your own head. Usually, what we call 'knowledge' refers to this first category.

The second kind of knowledge is obtained through the scientific method of observation, experiment, reasoning and analysis. Science is the result of these four elements. This system has a very strong base, because it is experienced directly. You can make deductions, draw conclusions and test them in front of your own eyes.

The third kind of knowledge is intuition: sudden insight, or connections being made without conscious logic. With this, you don't have scientific certainty; you cannot provide fully reasoned explanations, or demonstrate cause and effect clearly and consistently. Consequently, you can't place absolute trust in this kind of knowledge. Nevertheless it often proves useful. The approach used in Zen Buddhism attempts to evoke this third kind of knowledge.

In fact, all three kinds of knowledge can be useful, even though each form has its limitations. Even scientific knowledge is not perfect; there are many areas where theories and explanations are constantly changing and evolving. This is especially true in the area of understanding what is happening inside the human being. At present science, logic and the rational mind cannot fully comprehend this territory.

Or as the Persian mystic and poet Rumi phrased it in the thirteenth century:

There are two kind of intelligence; one acquired,
As a child in school memorises facts and concepts
From books and from what the teacher says,
Collecting information from the traditional sciences
As well as from the new sciences.

With such intelligence you rise in the world.
You get ranked ahead or behind others
In regard to your competence in retaining
    information.
You stroll with this intelligence
In and out of fields of knowledge, getting always more
    marks on your preserving tablets.

There is another kind of tablet,
One already completed and preserved inside you.
A spring overflowing its springbox.
A freshness in the centre of the chest.
This other intelligence does not turn yellow or
    stagnate.
It's fluid, and it doesn't move from outside to inside
    through the conduits
Of plumbing-learning.

This second knowing is a fountainhead
From within you, moving out.
The Essential Rumi translated by Coleman Barks with
       John Moyne, Penguin Books, 1999, p. 178.

Props

On the stage I often ask myself, 'Why do I have arms and hands?' I ask this because I don't know where to put them. I try shoving the hands into my pockets, or clasp them together, or put them on the waist. When actors are on the stage it is so difficult simply to stand or just to walk. If we can hold the back of a chair, or place our hand on the table, we somehow feel safe. In the same way if there is a prop (a flower or a cigarette, lipstick or teacup) at least we can grasp it in our hand and our arm has something to do. In real life we never think about having two arms and two hands, we never think about what to do with these things. And similarly when we have props on the stage, we don't feel uncomfortable about these two appendages. The legs are OK, we can stand on them; it is only the arms that are a problem.

In addition, when we have a prop we can feel some life in our body, and when we speak text we are not just a slave of the text, not just speaking words with a dead body. Instead, we can speak text with life, thanks to the props. For example, if I do the speech 'To be or not to be, that is the question . . .' with a flower in my hand, or a knife, it is a very different experience from doing it with empty hands. Because I hold the prop it makes me feel differently; the body is engaged and active. I am not only talking about simply holding props in a passive way, I am also talking about physical activities involving objects, such as knitting a sweater with wool, or drinking whisky, or getting undressed. And different props make you feel in different ways. And these different activities combined with the text make different stories for the public.

Whenever I act or direct, I try to use props while speaking. Drinking tea, wine, smoking, knitting, putting on make-up – any kind of activity. I do this because I don't like the actor just to stand or sit there and speak. The audience gets information from the ear (which is the text) but also through the eye. We can use movement to tell the story in theatre. Normally this involves sitting, standing and lying down. These are the basics. But if we use props, we can find more variety of body position. This allows the audience to see a greater range of physical action and response. Then it looks more like daily life, not some artificial theatrical situation.

But we have to be careful, because the audience cannot con-centrate on hearing and looking at the same time. So if there is movement during a very important phrase, the audience cannot focus on the meaning of the text.

Actors have to control this process. Even if we are speaking what we know to be a very important phrase, the audience will not stop looking at the visual. They don't know that the phrase is important. But if the actor suddenly stops the physical activity the audience gives up the visual dimension. All they can do is listen to the text. In this way they can focus on the deep meaning of the text. If we only want them to listen we stop the body. If we only want them to watch we stop the speech. This is how actors focus the situation and direct the attention of the audience.

With props and speech, the audience also makes a story with text and movement. If you do the 'To be or not to be' speech from *Hamlet* while picking up flowers, or alternatively, while destroying the flower, the public makes a different story. If you do the speech with a book in your hand it is another story again. Or with a wineglass, yet another story. But you must be careful. If you concentrate too much on the props while you are acting, the audience loses the sense of the phrases you are speaking. It isn't about trying to make the prop especially significant, but of finding the right prop. Also, sensing the right time to move with that prop and when to stop moving with it. Sometimes you stop the text and just have the activity of the props.

My Noh teacher, Master Okura, was very strict. He was the head of the school and felt responsible for properly maintaining the 600-year-old tradition he had inherited. If I carelessly put props on the floor, he would become very angry. He said that they are very important, more important to me than my own self, a great treasure that I should treat with respect. He said I had to think about them differently. He reminded me that I should never 'use' props; instead, I should attempt to produce a relationship between the props and myself. In fact, there were three possibilities: I could show my character through the props, or I could show the props through my actions, or I could try to show the relationship between myself and the props.

Costumes are important in the same way. They are not just beautiful designs, but an intrinsic part of the performance. Actors need to consider how to wear them; they should look as though they naturally belong to us. For this reason it is a good idea to wear them for extended periods before the opening night, or look at them for a long time in the mirror. Little by little the costume must become like our skin.

Creating life

Some time after the International Centre's return from Africa we created *Les Iks*, a performance based on the real-life situation of starving African villagers. The source material was a study by the anthropologist Colin Turnbull. In order to approach the life of those people, we did an exercise involving photographs of the villagers taken by Turnbull during a period of famine in the community. To begin encompassing their life, Peter asked us to imitate exactly the photos. The precise position of their bodies: their feet, the arms, the angle of the head. At first we created an exact imitation. Then we asked ourselves how we felt in that position, in order to gain some small sense of their life. It is not possible to analyse this intellectually, because we cannot know what it is like to be in their situation. Nor can imagination bridge this gap. But direct physical imitation gives us some kind of understanding of the inside. Then we extended the exercise into time. We had to create what happened before the moment in the photo, and discover how to arrive at the precise position shown in the image. Then we carried the exercise into the moment after the photo, discovering how to move from that place. We worked from the outside, in order to find some sense of the inner life.

In the theatre, most actors work from the inside to the outside; they start from the inner life of the character or the situation and subsequently try to discover the movement, and the vocal patterns, and the timing of the text. But at the same time, why not work from the outside? Working from the inside to the outside is simply current practice; it could change tomorrow. Analysing from the inside (psychology, character etc.) is not the only way to discover the piece. But there can be another problem with only working from the inside to the outside. Actors can often construct a strong inner existence, but sometimes they forget (or are unable) to make a clear exterior form. Sometimes the director says, 'At this moment I want you to be sad' and the actor protests that he or she is really feeling the emotion and the sadness is incredibly strong. And then the director replies, 'That's all very well, but I can't SEE it!' This is a classic problem.

OPERA AND DANCE

Over the past few years I have worked a lot with dancers and singers, creating and directing various productions. I never forget that the final aim of all theatre is the same: the performers move, and speak, with real human life. But to get to this destination, opera and dance take a different path from theatre.

Opera singers have a score. They already know exactly how to speak the text, since the score provides timing and melody as well as the words. The performers also have the main action and relationships set out in the score. They learn this from the outside. Then, as a director, I also provide some detailed movements and staging, like a choreographer. This also comes from the outside. And they have to find a way to make this choreography and score come alive. This is their search.

In the same way classical ballet dancers are given a fixed choreography, which they have to bring to life.

For a good singer or dancer, the question is how to create believable life inside the forms of their given choreography or score. The technical structure is like a kind of beautifully constructed box.

Ordinary dancers or singers just perform the box very well. It is correct and it looks good, but they don't fill it up with life.

Several years ago I met Jean Babilée (a French dancer who became famous after the Second World War as a result of his collaboration with Roland Petit. Petit created the original choreography for *Le Jeune Homme et la Mort* for Babilée).When I was talking with him, I asked what was the difference between an ordinary dancer and a good dancer. He replied, 'An ordinary dancer simply does the technique. A good dancer is a poet.' I then asked how a dancer could become a poet. His answer: 'It isn't something you can learn, you have to be born that way.' I don't quite agree with this idea that some people are born poets and others aren't. For me, everyone is born a poet and it is the demands of life (education, family and so on) that cause people to lose their quality of being poets.

In any event, singers and dancers need to find ways of filling their beautiful technical boxes with vivid life.

BRIDGES

One trick I use when I direct opera is to look for bridges. In the score there are the actual singing sections, plus many interludes where there is only music. Singers perform each of the vocal sections very well, but during the pauses they tend simply to wait for the next moment of singing. When that happens the life of that character stops. Also, the second section of the song doesn't develop from the first and each section of singing remains separate. But if there is no development between the sections you cannot represent life properly. This is not a question of simply filling the musical sections with activity, but to make a bridge between one section of singing and the next.

So I have to find bridges for the singers. Either emotional bridges, or physical bridges. In some cases I might suggest a psychological bridge. A thought process or an image that shifts them to what they will sing next. In other cases I might ask the singer to turn the head, or to sit down during the gap. Or drink tea, or peel potatoes. Then the personality can flow.

The main forms of Japanese classical theatre (Noh and Kabuki) work in exactly the same way as Western opera.

When I watch Japanese Kabuki actors, I am aware of their great technical skill.

Kabuki Theatre is the second style within the Japanese classical tradition. It came into existence in the seventeenth century and, like Noh, uses dance, singing, music and gorgeous costume in its presentation. Unlike Noh, however, it uses these elements to create vivid spectacle that dazzles the audience. The text focuses on melodramatic or romantic stories, often involving seductive courtesans, dispossessed Samurai and tragic lovers. All these are presented on a vividly painted stage, which alters according to the play (unlike the Noh Theatre set, which is identical for every single play). In addition, there are special effects and technical tricks (the Kabuki stage utilised the revolve for rapid set changes centuries before its use in the West). All this is designed to create strong, exciting, sensational performance, which excites and sways the audience.

In the Kabuki Theatre every single aspect of the performance is fixed by tradition. The exact movements of the body, the rhythmic patterns and intonations of the speech, and even the focusing of the eyes are all set down as formal choreography. The precise timing of pauses is choreographed, as is the posing of the body (called mie*) in moments of dramatic tension. L.M.*

They can do all the details of the action very well, because they have been learning the techniques of body and voice since they were six years old. In addition, they have learned the specific choreography for every moment of every scene. They can perform this with extraordinary skill. For example, take the following sequence:

There is a box on the stage. The actor approaches the box. He is afraid of what might be inside it, so he slowly opens it. He looks inside. He thinks he sees a dead body and is shocked. Then he has a second thought and looks inside again. He realises that it is a puppet, not the body of a real person. So he feels relieved and happy. There are three states: anticipation/fear, then surprise/shock, and finally relief and laughter. Kabuki actors can do the actions of this kind of scene very easily. When opening the box the actor can make a very beautiful pose and, using the exaggerated Kabuki style of expressing surprise, they can indicate the shock very well. The same with laughter and the relief.

But here again I saw the difference between a good actor and an ordinary actor. An ordinary actor just performs each separate action correctly with great technical skill, while a good actor makes some kind of bridge between two actions. In a sense the quality of acting shows in the transitions – in this case the ability to transform from fear to shock to relief. For the actor, the trick is to discover the right bridges, otherwise it doesn't work. But if he can find them, the life of the human being is built up and the performance becomes more alive for the audience.

For an actor, if he moves from anger to love he must find a path using bridges. But what we are discussing applies to all performance. Even when there is no clear psychological dimension, there is still a need for bridges. In ballet choreography there may be a sequence that goes from arabesque to step to jump. The question is how to move from A to B to C so that it looks natural and true. Professional dancers can do each element very well, but there is still a need for a bridge from arabesque to step to leap. Dancers also need to find paths.

It is necessary, too, for the path to be organic. If we have the right life psychologically or emotionally we can transform to the next physical moment. However, if we depend on our logical intelligence to find the path, there is a danger that it will be mechanical.

I often use the word 'tasting' when I ask people to sense how to transform from one moment to the next. This is a matter of feeling what comes next, without resorting to conscious decision-making. And it requires the body to be connected to the inner life. However, this is not always easy. As we know, actors can have great inner life, but they cannot assume it will automatically manifest in the body. Even when the psychology and the emotions are very alive, if they don't connect with the body it doesn't function for the audience. What we think and feel has to go into the body.

Organic transformation requires a good relationship between internal life and the body's life. How do you do this? I cannot suggest a single technique, but all performers should try to discover some way that works. The body needs to react to your internal life in a sensitive way, and there must be constant easy flow between inner and outer aspects. The body must be alive, the inner being must be alive, but there must also be flow between the two.

PREPARATION TRICKS

There is a story about a well-known Kabuki actor called Tamasaburo Bando. One day he gave a performance, and afterwards people came up and told him that it was fantastic, quite brilliant. The other actors asked him what had happened and he said, 'Yesterday I saw a beautiful painting of my character and I stood in front of that painting for three hours. Somehow, today I played that painting.' The body somehow can absorb that kind of rich information.

In the Kabuki Theatre all women's parts are played by male actors called *onnagata*. An old trick was for the actor to put his hand in cold water before going on stage, so that when the actor playing the male role took the hand it would feel cold. And the hero would think, 'Ah, the poor woman, I want to warm her hand.' In this way affection towards women characters is created.

There are many ways to help actors find the life of the play. For example, when we were working on *The Mahabharata*, the entire company went to India. We went to Hindu temples, met various gurus, watched Kathakali performances and generally started to sense daily life on the subcontinent. Even in Paris, Brook showed us pictures, played music, invited experts to talk, in order to help us become more aware of Indian culture. In the same way we spent three months observing patients and doctors in the hospital as preparation for *The Man Who*. And for *Tierno Bokar* we went to Fez in North Africa for the rehearsal period. It isn't an intellectual method, but operates via direct physical experience: seeing, hearing, visiting, tasting. In this way something starts cooking deep inside the actor, something based on real life. The preparation is not about how to speak or how to move. Instead, Brook brings us to the world of the play through direct physical experience.

People often ask me what I have learned from Peter Brook. There is no easy answer. When I was writing this book I asked Peter, 'What have I learned from you? I need to put this information in the book.' He answered, 'Just leave two blank pages.'

When I started with the International Centre there were improvisation exercises every day. This was a problem for me since I had no experience with improvisation, so all I could do was try to use the techniques I had learned from the Japanese classical theatre. After a month or so Peter asked me not to use anything from my Japanese background. Since these elements were forbidden, I didn't know what to do in improvisation, but in the end this instruction was very valuable. I had to find another way. By removing all that is unnecessary and by examining everything that is superficially obvious, such as 'I am Japanese', my name is 'Yoshi Oida', 'I am so and so years old', he helped me remove the blocks and disguises. He did not tell me what I should do; he only removed the inessential. In this way I began to discover freedom.

Over time, Peter's work has become more and more radical and minimalist, which in fact makes the actor's work more difficult.

At the beginning of the rehearsal process for *Tierno Bokar* we had a lot of stories and on the stage a multitude of objects. During the rehearsal Peter took them away one by one. The text and the visual elements gradually became simpler and simpler. This is hard for actors since we have to search for a strong expression without any element of demonstrating. Naturally, that doesn't mean we just wandered around the stage doing nothing. Instead, we began by rehearsing to the maximum, then the excess was taken away piece by piece. When you perform in this way you have to concentrate fully on the smallest details and internal processes. It is essential that you are lively in the innermost part and that you develop a maximum concentration on the essential. Of course, this inner life is invisible, but it still depends on how you express it.

This is the process the artist Matisse used in drawing. He would draw the full image, then erase a large number of strokes until he found the minimum required to communicate what he wanted.

THE AUDIENCE

In rehearsals, even when a run-through goes very well, we must remember that this is not the final thing. Theatre without an audience doesn't exist. For this reason it is useful to invite an audience, preferably a group of people from outside the theatre profession. Without an audience actors can't really comprehend what they are doing. Once I am in front of an audience, I can understand how to play: tempo, energy, action, everything. Something essential but invisible comes from the audience and there is a kind of instinct that allows actors to sense this. In fact, normal rehearsals are just preparations, which then allow us to discover something else in front of the spectators. The final decision cannot appear until they have been involved. Rehearsals are about collecting materials for acting. If I do the same thing I did in the rehearsals when the audience is present it's wrong. I must somehow develop the work once I am with an audience. In fact, normal rehearsals are the preparation for the open rehearsal. The audience acts like a mirror to the work, reflecting back what is happening.

Since no one can ever know how a show is going until the public comes in, many directors schedule open rehearsals. However, there are different ways for them to observe the audience's reactions. Some directors watch them, checking responses to various moments. Other directors prefer to feel the audience, becoming a part of it, sensing and sharing their reactions.

When we did *Tierno Bokar*, rehearsals started at the beginning of 2004. After three months of preparation and rehearsal, the première took place in Germany in July. However, the work of the company was not finished at the première; it continued to develop for the entire run. During the Paris season of the show we had weekly rehearsals, which allowed Peter to modify the performance again and again. This way the performance can stay lively.

When I direct, I try to follow his method. I try to learn from the audience. And so I keep working on the show throughout the run, sometimes right up to the last night.

In April 1990 I directed a production of *Endgame* by Samuel Beckett. The whole play is a conflict between Ham and Clov. They are always arguing and fighting, but suddenly, in the middle of the play, Ham starts a long speech, talking about his novel. While I was directing, I couldn't understand why this element appeared so suddenly and I had no idea of how to approach the scene. We couldn't cut the text, so I just asked the actor to speak the words. When we held an open rehearsal, in order to get the reactions of the audience, I asked people what they felt. Many people said that the most marvellous moment was when Ham was telling this story. Which shows that Beckett is a great writer and, at the same time, that you can never understand a play through reading the text in your head. You have to speak and you have to see; then you can understand. You cannot understand a play until you have an audience.

OTHER TRICKS

There are a number of different methods directors can use to encourage life during rehearsals. When I directed *Madame de Sade* (by Yukio Mishima), I started in my usual way, with physical activity and improvisation. I placed furniture in the space, as if it were a rococo salon, and asked the actors to improvise. Their first question was, 'Where is the audience?' They were already thinking in terms of the final staging.

The company found it difficult to do pure improvisation with text and action. They felt they could not move until they had all the details of psychological motivation and could not even begin to learn the text without the psychological background.

I feel it is important to respect different working methods, so the actors invited a psychiatrist to the rehearsal to help them understand the psychological background to the play. I was happy to accept his presence, since I wanted to help the actors in any way I could. And I know it is always useful to understand deeply human psychology. But at the same time there is a danger of becoming prisoner of intellectual analysis, especially when trying to understand your own character. It doesn't allow you any space to discover.

In terms of acting, I feel that the human being has such a mysterious beauty. It is not always logical or consistent. Even in real life, you can tell your lover to leave, but when he or she has gone, you ask yourself why you said those things. You didn't really want them to go. Maybe a psychologist can analyse why you did this strange thing, but I am not sure his answer is correct. You always do odd things and you never really understand why you do them. That is why it is so interesting to play various characters and, through them, to discover how mysterious human life is.

The great secret of directing is patience. It is not about commanding or instructing an actor, but about exchanging ideas in order to discover something together. Each actor has a vast potential of poetry and creativity, but only when this energy flows freely can something interesting and new develop. When people think they are always right about what they do and say, they don't need to be involved in theatre any more. As the character Tierno Bokar says in the play of the same name, 'There are three truths: my truth, your truth and the truth.' In the same way the director and the actor work together to create this third type of reality.

There were three famous Shoguns in Japanese history, who lived around the turn of the seventeenth century. Each of them wanted to hear a nightingale sing. The first one, Nobunaga, said, 'If the nightingale doesn't sing, kill it.' The second one, Hideyoshi, said, 'If the nightingale doesn't sing, I'll force it to.' The third one was Ieyasu. He said, 'If the nightingale doesn't sing, I'll just wait until he is ready to perform.' You can think about this in terms of rehearsal. Sometimes you say, 'If I can't get what I want, I'll just give up.' Or you might say, 'If I can't get what I want, I'll force myself to continue until it happens.' Or you could follow the third option: 'If I can't get what I want I'll just wait patiently until something changes.' In fact, all three approaches are necessary. You have to shift between these tactics according to the situation.

3 Entering the Theatre

When I was a child of eight or nine, I loved going to the theatre. I insisted on going as often as possible, even sneaking away from school in order to see matinée performances, usually of some kind of popular entertainment. And I loved to stand at the very front of the audience, right at the edge of the stage. Before the show began I would lift the curtain and poke my head into the stage space. Technicians were running around, changing the set, placing the props and checking details. Eventually the technicians would spot me and tell me to go back to the other side of the curtain. I didn't want to obey, since I wanted to understand how the magic of the stage was created.

One of the reasons I wanted to become an actor was so that I could be part of that hidden world, rather than sitting out in front just watching it. I wanted to enter the theatre through the stage door rather than via the public foyer. For me, the stage door was the mysterious entrance to another reality.

When you enter a Japanese theatre through the artists' entrance, you will see a small wooden construction placed high on the wall. There are twisted ropes, and hanging paper shapes, and an array of miniature bowls and flasks, containing water, rice wine, salt and uncooked rice. This is a miniature Shinto shrine and it exists in all Japanese theatre buildings, even the ones being constructed today. Every day, when the actors come to the theatre, they stop in front of the shrine and make a short prayer, asking that no accidents occur and that the show goes well. According to tradition, the actors also make an offering of rice wine to the shrine on the dates of the première, the middle show and the final performance.

In the Kabuki Theatre there is another special practice. Every day, when the actor (in the Kabuki Theatre all actors are male) leaves his house to go to the theatre, his wife stands in the doorway watching him leave and makes a brief ceremony. She takes a short iron blade and a piece of hard stone, and strikes them together until sparks fly out. She does this twice as he departs. The sparks symbolise exorcism and purification.

Actors are modern people living in a modern world, and we want to create theatre that is original and ground-breaking. Yet at the same time there is something archaic in the way we think of our craft. In Britain, the play *Macbeth* is seen as very bad luck; most actors will never speak the title (referring to it as the Scottish Play) and many refuse to act in it for fear of coming to harm. In France the colour green is bad luck and is never used in costumes. There is the same association in Italy with the colour purple.

There is an eighteenth-century Kabuki play called *Yotsuya Kaidan* (*The Ghost Story of Yotsuya*) based on the real-life story of a woman who was killed by her husband. After her death, her ghost returned to haunt and torment the husband, who was eventually driven mad. Because this play involved someone who had actually lived, every time it is performed the entire Kabuki company goes to the shrine containing her grave, before starting rehearsals, to pray for her and to ask that no accidents occur. In the summer of 2005 I performed a modern version of this play in Japan (using the original Kabuki script) and our entire company, including the German director, went to the cemetery and offered prayers.

Early in the history of Noh theatre (more than 600 years ago) the government gave actors the right to perform certain religious rituals. Up to that point in history the actors were mainly popular entertainers and storytellers, and perceived as very low class. By performing rituals the status of the Noh actors was raised and their art came to be taken more seriously. Nowadays, when we look at Noh Theatre, it all appears very ritualistic, but that is a matter of performing style. In fact, most Noh plays are dramatic rather than religious in nature. With one exception: the Noh play called *Okina* is actually a genuine ritual, one that pre-dates the foundation of the Noh Theatre tradition. It is a ceremony for the spirits of the sky and the earth. One mask (Okina) is the god of the sky and the other mask (Sambasu) is the god of the earth.

Traditionally, when actors enacted these two roles they took their preparation very seriously. For the week preceding the performance, they remained in their own huts. Women were not permitted to enter this retreat, not even to provide food. The men had to prepare their own, vegetarian, food – no contact at all with women. Every morning and evening they had to purify themselves by bathing in cold water. Today, I don't know how many modern Noh actors still follow this tradition, but the play itself is still the most important performance for Noh actors because they are not 'acting'; they are undertaking a genuine ritual.

I often ask myself if this kind of careful preparation is useful, not just for ritual but for the performer's life. For example, are sexual relations positive, or negative, or irrelevant? The same with food. But there is another factor: Noh performances take place only once, so the actor can focus his preparation for a single date. But how can I do this kind of purification when I have to do a show every single night for six months? I once heard that Tatsumi Hijikata, the co-founder of Butoh, used to fast for ten days prior to a performance, but again that was for a single performance, not a season.

THE BODY AS A TEMPLE

Many cultures construct temple buildings: special places where visitors come to have emotional and spiritual experiences. Temple buildings in Asia are often constructed as miniature versions of the larger world. In a sense, the body is the same: a world in itself and the site of extraordinary experiences. And like a temple we must keep the structure clean and pure. This requires good-quality food and appropriate clothing, and an awareness that we should treat the edifice with respect. There is another way in which we can view our body as a temple. Most sacred buildings have a special area, a sanctum deep inside, where spiritual powers live or appear. People pray to these powers for help. In the same way we can view our body as containing energies that enable us to achieve our aims.

As well as a temple, our body is also our friend. It should be treated with great love and respect. After all, we share death and life with it, and it is always present in our moments of greatest joy and deepest suffering. We shouldn't mistreat it, or ask it to engage in unpleasant actions just because we are bored. It isn't kind to prostitute it, or embellish it in an exaggerated way simply to please our vanity. We mustn't ask it to degrade itself. If we treat the body as a space for excess, or crude actions, it has to work to eliminate every single piece of rubbish and pollution deposited there. Eventually it loses its purity and its spiritual energy. If we persist in living this way, we are insulting our body. The body is the home of the actor and the territory where all experience lives: pleasure, pain, sadness and joy.

We could also view the body as our servant; after all, if we want to go somewhere, it takes us to our destination. And it is grateful for the interesting experiences we ordain. If we place our body on top of a Russian mountain, or on horseback, or in the sea, it is very happy. It is equally delighted if we give it newly baked bread or a cup of freshly brewed coffee. And while it enjoys being decorated with jewellery or make-up in ways that enhance its actual beauty, it won't complain if we dress it in torn old rags (even though it isn't actually very pleased with our choice). We could say that the body is a perfect servant, even a slave, but in fact it is a friend . . . and none of us will find a better partner anywhere in the world.

It is thanks to their bodies that remarkable people have achieved their aims. Great individuals, prophets, mystics, poets, actors, painters, athletes, political leaders, fighters, saints have all understood the importance of the body and have carved their path through the body's actions. If the body is not in activity, the individual is not engaged. This is another reason why we should train our body every single day. Physical exercises are valuable for many reasons, not just a strong physique or enhanced inner energy. And we should feel affection towards our body.

However, we mustn't get confused; love for our body should not become the centre of our personal existence. It must not become attached to our ego, or a source of narcissism. While everyone's body can be viewed as a temple, the actor's body is a temple for the public. It must become the site of events that provide wonderful sensations and emotions for other people.

In esoteric Shinto there is an exercise that you do every morning: you face your own image in the mirror, and you bow and say 'Thank you very much' to your body. This is because while you were sleeping, your body continued breathing, and digesting, and processing whatever you have taken in. It has been working all the time. You can sleep, but the body never stops, never has a rest, or takes a vacation. When you bow every day in this way, you start to feel another sensation towards your body. Most people agree that we have both a body and some kind of internal spirit or energy. This exercise helps them have a good relationship with each other; the body is acknowledged as a kind of object that supports the spirit.

PREPARATION FOR THE SHOW

Very few performers come straight from the streets, get changed and go directly on to the stage. There seems to be a need for a period of preparation. In Indian Kathakali the actors receive massage for one hour before performing. Perhaps this is similar to what some

Western dancers do before going on stage, or perhaps it has a deeper meaning. I don't know. In the Japanese classical theatre (including both Noh and Kabuki) the actors also bow formally to each other in the dressing room.

Like most actors, I prefer to do thirty minutes of physical exercise before each performance, so that the body starts to come alive and the energy begins to flow. In addition, when I am performing as part of a company, I don't want to encounter the other actors for the first time on the stage during the performance; we need some kind of contact before we meet there. So it is useful to do our exercises together. If, for any reason, the group exercises don't occur, we meet anyway, not just to say hello to each other, but to make contact with each other as performers.

For me, these three elements of preparation are very important: physical awakening, internal energy awakening and the creation of some sort of unity among the performers. The difficulty with doing physical exercises as part of your preparation is judging them accurately. If you work too hard, you become tired and find you have no physical energy left when you enter the stage. But too much relaxation and calming is equally unproductive; you become sleepy and not sufficiently alive on stage. On the stage it is a sort of game that you are playing. For this reason joy and energy, allied with concentration and calmness, is the ideal. You need both aspects. And it isn't easy to create a preparation that works at both extremes.

It is also important to understand what we mean when people say you need to 'relax' on the stage. Theatrical relaxation must be free but at the same time strong and concentrated: good quality, with a solid strong energy, and a body that is alive and dynamic. *In this context, it is interesting to note that the original meaning of the verb 'to relax' is 'to loosen', or 'to free from legal restraint', or 'to make less strict'* (Oxford Concise Dictionary of English Etymology). *It is about release, rather than softening or de-energising. L.M.*

In addition, the exact programme of preparation is a difficult thing to formulate; it depends on what kind of performance you are doing. If it is a very dynamic show, you have to do dynamic exercises in order to evoke energy. But if it is a very quiet, concentrated show you have to calm down the energy.

Part of your preparation also involves becoming attuned to your performing space. You need to understand instinctively the size of the theatre and how your acting energy can fill that physical space. When I lead preparation exercises for the company before a show, I always prefer to do them on the actual stage rather than a rehearsal room. Therefore, without knowing, little by little, the actors begin to understand the theatre's interior space.

You can do the same thing with the voice, tuning it to the space. Standing on the stage the actor speaks his own text and another actor listens from the audience. Then from both sides you can feel how strong your voice needs to be, or how minimal. It isn't only a case of you understanding how to do your speech, but through listening to another actor's voice you can understand how the voice actually arrives in the audience. Again, this is an instinctive understanding, it doesn't require a logical analysis. By doing your warm-up in the actual performing space, you are helping the other instinctive intelligence to connect to the environment.

Rituals of preparation

Over the years, artists tend to develop rituals of preparation. Some individuals might sing while getting dressed, or walk up and down in the corridor, or meditate in their own way. Whatever helps each particular actor is fine. In fact, all of these are useful ways of drawing a line between ordinary life and the world of the performance. The act of putting on stage make-up can also help the performers separate themselves from their daily existence.

When I was a young man working in modern theatre in Japan, all the actors did their own make-up. I used to watch what other people were doing. I noticed that one man who had very thin eyebrows would draw them in much thicker, while someone else who had a flat nose would add putty to build it up to a stronger shape. So I began to understand the inferiority complexes of those individuals. In a way, they wanted to be perfect, so with make-up they tried to make adjustments. For me the thin eyebrows looked fine on the worried actor, but for him it was a defect. Actors often reveal their fears and their weak points when they make choices about their appearance. If they feel they are too short they want to wear high heels. If they feel their face is fat, they do a lot of shading. On the stage actors try to transform themselves into the being that they adulate. They want to fit some kind of ideal of beauty or attractiveness, or repair reality.

But sometimes other things happen through make-up. Philippe Adrien (a well-known French director) phoned a famous make-up artist called Reiko Kruk. He said, 'We are rehearsing *Waiting for Godot*, but something is missing. Maybe the two actors are too young. Can you do something?' Reiko did not give the actors ageing make-up; instead, she created a false nose for one of them. Suddenly his performance became much better. So the director asked the artist to give the other main actor a false nose as well and his acting also improved. The third actor, who was playing Pozzo, watched these events and asked if he could have a nose too. So in the end three out of the four characters had false noses and the performance went very well.

About fifty years ago a Japanese actor played a major role in one of Yukio Mishima's plays called *Roku Meikan (The Castle of Rokumei)*. His role was that of an honourable politician, a member of the opposition to the government. But in fact he was too young to play that role, since he was only in his early thirties. The director tried very hard, but nothing seemed to work. The company was on the edge of despair. But at the dress rehearsal he was given the moustache for his character and suddenly it all fell into place.

Make-up changes the outside, but a mask enables you to go even further with this transformation. Make-up adheres to your skin and follows the movements of the face muscles. Your own movements and expressions can be seen through it. But with a mask the situation is different; the 'skin' surface of the mask (especially the wooden ones used in Noh Theatre) sits two or three centimetres away from your own skin, which is a significant distance. In addition it does not move when your face changes expression. It has its own existence, which the actor accepts and transforms into.

There is an old tradition that the night before a performance the actor will take the mask to his house and sleep with it. The two faces share the same bed.

My Noh teacher's passion was collecting old masks, which he kept in his house. He was worried about the danger of fire. (*Since traditional Japanese houses are made of wood and paper, the risk of burning is very high. L.M.*) Some of these masks were classified as national treasures. I said to him, 'Why don't you ask about keeping them in a museum?' He said, 'If you leave a mask in a museum, the mask dies. The mask must go on the stage from time to time to live as a character and be seen by an audience. Otherwise they lose their life and just become objects. A mask is not an object.'

I felt the same thing when I saw a painting by El Greco in the Prado museum in Madrid. It did not touch me. Then I went to a small town near Madrid, where there was another painting by El Greco, this time housed in a church. Here the painting was wonderful. These objects need the existence for which they were made; the masks were made for the stage, the paintings were created for a church. When they are moved to a museum they become mere objects for viewing and the invisible part of that art disappears.

In her book entitled Colour *(Hodder & Stoughton, 2002), Victoria Finlay describes a museum in Cremona, which houses several rare antique violins, including one by Stradivarius. Although they are carefully protected in hermetically sealed, air-conditioned display cases, they must be removed every day and played by a violinist. Otherwise they will lose their ability to vibrate properly and simply become carved wooden shapes.*

Apparently, after a major restoration it can take a violin a month or more to return to concert standard. L.M.

With a mask your outside changes very strongly and this makes your inside also change. But the opposite, too, can occur. Sometimes if you change your inside very strongly it can somehow alter the outside, but not through obvious, visible action.

On occasion, when teaching workshops, I ask people to choose one of three colours: yellow, blue or red. Then I ask them to try to unify with that colour. Not to perform it, but without moving to try to unify themselves with it. Then I ask other people to try to guess which one it is. It is never one hundred per cent correct, but very often others can guess which colour is the focus. That means that your invisible appearance is somehow different and other people can see it. This is the work of the actor's imagination.

In Japanese Noh Theatre, the sounds that a drummer makes are not improvisations; every beat and pause is set by a score. Curiously enough, the scores to express 'snow falling' and 'heavy rain' are identical. If an average musician plays these two scores there is no difference; it is simply sound. But if a good musician plays this musical construction the audience will feel 'Oh, this is the sound of snow', or 'This is the sound of falling rain'. Somehow the audience senses something different and this difference seems to come through the imagination of the drummer.

A few years ago the famous Kabuki actor Nakamura Utaemon died. He was renowned for his portrayals of sensitive and beautiful young women, which he continued to perform into his extreme old age. Of course, he wore a wig and make-up as part of the role, but these did not hide the lines and sagging features. Yet somehow when he performed, you forgot you were watching an old man; you only saw the beautiful young princess. Between his skill and the power of his internal transformation, he became what he was not. L.M.

This is the magic of performance. Logically, when you act, the body that appears on the stage should be the same as the one you saw in the dressing-room mirror; your outside cannot actually change. But when you start to act from the inside with a strong imagination, the public sees something different from the realistic reflection. When you are playing on the stage, you are working with something very familiar: your own face and your own body. But then something different occurs. Something fundamental changes.

4 In the Wings

It is nearly time to begin the show. I finish putting on my costume and go to the backstage area. The first thing I do is to sneak a look at the audience. At the Bouffes du Nord Theatre in Paris there is a little hole in the door I can peep through, or in other theatres I steal a glance through the curtains. I want to know what kind of people I will be spending time with: young, old, lively or serious.

I also need to sense how I should enter in terms of their energy. This is something I learned from the precepts of Zeami.

Motokiyo Zeami (AD 1363–1443) is a major figure in Japanese theatre history, being responsible for the creation of Noh Theatre. He welded together two earlier styles of performance, Sarugaku and Dengaku. Sarugaku (literally 'monkey music') was a form of popular entertainment using tricks, comedy and acrobatics. Dengaku ('field music') had its origin in the songs and dances that were performed as part of agricultural ritual.

As this new art emerged, Zeami refined its subject matter, style of presentation and acting techniques. In order to pass on his theatrical insights to following generations of actors he wrote several treatises. These were handed down in secret among the families of the Noh Theatre. Only in 1908, when a collection of these writings accidentally appeared in a second-hand bookshop, did the information become available to the general public. Although Zeami's books were written hundreds of years ago, his

ideas are fascinating and completely relevant to modern (and Western)
actors. They are available in English translation. L.M.

Zeami used the concepts of yin and yang extensively in his work,
and said that when your audience is in the state of 'yin', you have to
play 'yang', and when the audience is 'yang', you have to play 'yin'.
If the audience is low energy you have to wake them up, but when
they are too agitated you have to calm them down. The moment
when you enter the stage, you must feel the life of the public, which
is not the same as the life of an individual. The whole group together
makes a single life and this is what you must catch.

This doesn't just apply at the beginning of the play. When I was
performing in *The Mahabharata*, a nine-hour marathon, I didn't
actually enter the stage until the play had already been running for
an hour. I watched the performance from the audience and observed
what was happening. If the tempo was a bit slow or heavy, I knew I
had to bring more energy with my entrance. Or if it were too
entertaining and funny, I tried to enter in a serious way in order to
calm things down.

While waiting in the wings, I look around to see the other actors;
some of them are chatting away to each other, some are meditating,
some are walking up and down. For myself I take two or three deep
breaths and put my body into the posture of the character.

MIRROR ROOM

In the Noh Theatre there are two different spaces for preparation.
There is the dressing room backstage where the actor puts on the
costume. But there is also another room in the wings called the
'mirror room' (*kagami-no-ma*), a small room just behind the curtain
leading to the stage, which is for transformation into character.
Before a performance the actor holds the mask between his hands
for a while, looking at the face that will be performing. He bows to

it in respect and puts it on his face. He then sits looking at his image in the mirror and lets what he sees change his inside. He becomes the mask.

When you put on the costume and mask, you look at yourself and try to understand what kind of person you are. In the mirror you can see your personality from the outside and you register its physical form. And while you are looking at the outside of your self, you try to understand that character. Little by little you 'cook' yourself, adjusting the inside and the outside so that they harmonise. It's like a box; you see this box and you try to understand what is inside it.

But even with the mirror you never really know what you look like. You see the mask and the costume, but they are static. And you only see yourself from the front. Once you begin to move on stage, turning and shifting, it becomes something different. This is part of the magic of performance.

There is the same problem with the voice. You cannot hear yourself in the same way as the audience hears you, since half of the sound you hear comes from outside, but the other half is heard internally. There are resonances inside your own skull, which the audience does not hear. In addition, when your voice goes to the audience it travels through the air and changes by the time it reaches them. You can never hear your voice in the same way as the audience does. This is another reason why I ask other actors to listen to me speak on the stage as part of my warm-up. They can hear what the audience actually receives and help me make adjustments.

Despite these problems the actor should try to understand what the audience is seeing and experiencing.

When I first came to Europe, my Noh teacher said to me, 'You must learn *ri-ken-no-ken*.' The direct translation is 'distance-seeing' and the concept was originally created by Zeami. It means that when you act on the stage, you must observe what you are doing with the external eye. If you can do this, you can experience a shared world between you and the audience.

RI-KEN-NO-KEN

Somewhere between the subjective and objective, another element is born. The artistic sense is not from inside or from outside. As an actor you look at every aspect of yourself (thought, emotion, movement) from the inside, but at the same time you look at your image from the outside. Then you can act. When you do this something emerges, a strange psychological state. This phenomenon is beyond logical explanation. It has no logic, no words, no intelligence, but with experience you will start to understand.

When I started working with Peter Brook I tried to discover *ri-ken-no-ken*. Every day there were a lot of improvisations: situation, character or movement. But when I went into an improvisation, I was totally involved in using my imagination and body to make things. And I forgot about *ri-ken-no-ken*, because I was too closely involved. But when I tried to look at myself from the outside I couldn't act at all, because I was always controlling what I was doing. It seemed impossible to reconcile the two points of view.

But one day, when I was in a good state while improvising, I suddenly found I was looking at myself from the outside, while at the same time being fully involved with the improvisation situation. It was such a surprise. Until then I had always thought that *ri-ken-no-ken* was from the audience's actual point of view, that is, from the front. But at that moment I discovered that in fact I was looking at myself from the rear; seeing myself from high up and behind.

When I went back to Japan and saw my teacher, I said, '*Ri-ken-no-ken* is not looking at myself from the front, but from the rear.' And he said, 'That's it!'

But there is a danger in this kind of work; if you try too hard to look at yourself, you cannot become the character. Your emotions will not be true, and your movements will be controlled by your intelligence and will create a cold performance. This isn't useful, because you do have to live the role completely. On the other hand if you go too far inside the character it can lead you into a trance-like state, which is equally unhelpful. In addition, when you do this it is easy to lose awareness of the audience and perform only for your own satisfaction. This in turn creates a barrier between you and the audience, which is not something you want. Instead, you want to maintain a natural, dynamic flow between you and the public.

A Samurai warrior once asked a Zen Master about where he should place his perception and concentration. The Master replied, 'Not on the tip of your attacker's sword and not on the tip of your own. You should also not focus on your hands, or the movement of your attacker's feet. Instead, you should focus everywhere and nowhere at the same time, and keep your perception moving. Like a mirror, which reflects everything, but fixes on nothing.'

The first time I saw a video of my acting I was shocked and horrified. I instantly fell into total despair. I had thought I was acting very well, but when I saw the video I discovered I was acting really, really badly. Since then I have tried to develop *ri-ken-no-ken*. I cannot do it all the time, but occasionally I touch it. When that happens, and I see a video of my stage performance at that moment, I can recognise that what I see is accurate. I observe an action on the screen, and I say to myself, 'Yes. That's what I did at that moment.' This means that while I was acting I was also unconsciously observing my actions and listening to my words. But I do wonder where the ear and eye are located that are observing my performance.

Nowadays I am interested in doing this kind of observation in my daily life as well. Why? Maybe because I don't want to become a simple slave of habit, doing the same actions over and over again without awareness. Or maybe because for me life is like theatre. Or perhaps there is a simpler reason – even as an old man I want to try to understand much more about how we function in our lives. So, while walking down the street, or sitting in the metro, or meeting people, I am try to remain aware that somebody else (which is also me) is watching and listening. Even when my emotions are involved,

I attempt to do the same. But in real life it is much more difficult to do than on the stage. In fact, I usually forget to watch. But I really would like to do it as much as possible.

As well as telling me to aim for *ri-ken-no-ken*, my Master gave me a further piece of advice: 'When you go to Europe don't think about your own success. Instead of trying to find ways to act well, try to think about how you can help other people.'

When I was young I learned a lot and I tried very hard to show it, so other actors hated to be my partner. But eventually I questioned why I did this; it is meaningless and made me feel bad, because I was not respecting relationships with other people. All of us have to learn how to work with other people and to create a genuine exchange with them.

Sometimes I have to work with somebody I dislike. Maybe that person is a liar, or spiteful, or very selfish. Yet somehow we have to make a good performance together, so I must find some kind of positive relationship. So I try to see behind that negative behaviour and horrible attitude to the essential person. I believe that every person in the world is fundamentally beautiful, but that life itself can be very hard. When people are facing a difficult time it can lead them to distortion, or ugly behaviour. But this behaviour is adaptation to the circumstances of living, not a reflection of their true nature, which is always beautiful. So I try to see beyond the negative surface to the beauty within.

In daily life we should also try to see beyond the surface. In general, if we really want to have good relations with another person we shouldn't look at the face. Of course, we look at the eyes and the expression, but instead of staying on the surface, we should try to go inside to the heart. Otherwise our relationships with other people are surface relationships, not deep human relationships. It is true that in daily life we have many surface relationships, with the bank teller, the supermarket checkout person and so on. But in these cases we are looking at other people only for ourselves, for how they affect us, how they meet our needs. We don't go deep inside to see who they are themselves. In Japanese there are two different verbs for 'to look'; '*kan*' and '*ken*'. '*Ken*' is to look at the outside, while '*kan*' is to look at the inside.

> *When Yoshi was rehearsing his production of* Curlew River *in Rouen, he used the following exercise as part of the preparation for the singers.*
>
> *Walk up to another performer, stop, look deep inside that person and make a personal gesture of greeting. It can be any kind of gesture; you can bow, or bring your hands to your heart. It doesn't have to be a gesture that is found anywhere in the real world. If you choose to shake hands, imagine that you are not only grasping a part of the actor's anatomy; you shake your hand deep inside the other person. L.M.*

Or step up to another actor and look at him or her. When you breathe out, feel that you are really entering the other person. When you breathe in, let the other person enter you. Not just a surface exchange of gestures or information, it is both of you looking deeper into each other – a different kind of relation.

In daily life when we shake hands it's just a social habit. We don't care. In the same way, once we know someone and become familiar with their face, we don't really look at them any more. We don't try to understand how our friend is today by looking beyond the face. In fact, a person's face is almost identical from day to day, but inside is not the same.

I once met a clairvoyant in Japan and she told me that I would never be a star. She said that I would be able to help other people, but not become a star. I was very disappointed, but I have never forgotten what she said. And when I am acting, I am always asking, 'How can I make other people free with me? How can I enable them to perform better?' In the same way when I direct, I don't push my ideas too much. Instead, I find great pleasure in hearing people say to the actors, or dancers, or singers 'That was the best performance in your career', or 'You are working much better now'. For me, this is a greater pleasure than realising my own ideas. So when I direct, I always ask myself how I can make the performers look good for the audience, or how do I enable them to work well.

Now I am standing in the wings, waiting. People often ask me if I get stage fright before a show. When I was young I got really nervous: my heart beat fast and my mouth went dry. But why? I suppose that I wanted to be really good on the stage and hoped that the audience would like me. To calm myself down, I would breathe as deeply as I could with my eyes closed. In the same way I would stand in front of the mirror, and look at myself and say, 'I am a good actor. I am a good actor . . .' Trying to hypnotise myself, so that on the stage, I would have less fear and slightly more confidence.

Now I think about it differently. I have done my ordinary daily preparation and been careful how I treat my body. I have learned my text, researched the play, rehearsed and warmed up, put on my costume and make-up. I have attempted to work with *ri-ken-no-ken* and a real perception of my fellow actors. I have put my body into the shape of my character. And now? Will it work? Nobody can be certain. There is no guarantee that all this preparation will create a good performance. Yesterday might have been good, but there is no way of knowing what will happen today. I have to keep my fingers crossed. Good acting happens when the god of acting comes into me on the stage. If it doesn't come in, I can still deliver the *mise-en-scène*, but I cannot get the same satisfaction. But I don't know how to make the god of acting turn up every time. So I pray, 'Please, God of Theatre, come into me today.' Then I step on to the stage. The audience is waiting.

In the Sistine chapel is Michelangelo's famous painting of God creating Adam. The moment of creation itself is when the two outstretched hands almost make contact.

5   On the Stage

There are two or three hours of performance ahead of me. How do I get through them? By following a kind of map or itinerary. And this is what the rehearsal process is actually about: creating a good map. You rehearse in order to define the *mise-en-scène*, using the elements of space, character, action and thought. Then you follow this design from moment to moment as you perform. But each of these four elements is quite complex.

THE SPACE

For audiences, the theatre space itself can be very exciting. Unless you know exactly how the auditorium is set up, you never really know what space you will be entering. Maybe it will be a traditional proscenium arch theatre, but will it have a curtain? With more modern theatres there is a variety of stage forms and in some theatres the physical set-up can change from show to show. Will it be a thrust stage with the audience on three sides, or completely in the round? Will there be seats at many levels, or maybe no seats at all?

In Japanese classical theatre these elements are all fixed by tradition. The Noh Theatre stage was originally an outdoor platform made of wood, usually built within the precincts of a Shinto shrine. It later moved indoors and the audience was placed in fixed seating to the front and stage-right side of the auditorium. The stage itself has retained a number of features from its original outdoor setting. The main performing area is a raised wooden platform, usually between six to ten metres square in size. Despite being indoors, the stage is covered by a roof, and there is also a raised bridge-walkway (the hashigakari*) as the main entrance to the performing area. This begins in the stage-right wings, and connects to the right side of the performing square. The stage platform itself is open on three sides and backed by a wall at the rear. On the stage left there is a short wall at the rear, with a low door set into it, then this side also becomes open. The Noh stage is effectively a three-sided thrust stage, with the audience sitting on two sides.*

In the Noh Theatre there are two points of entry for performers. The chorus enters from the low door on stage left (which requires them to bend down in order to enter), while the musicians enter via the hashigakari *bridge. After these performers are in position, the first actor appears at the beginning of the* hashigakari *and starts the journey of the play. The actors commence their performance on the* hashigakari*, but the main drama is carried out on the stage platform.*

In the early Noh theatres, the hashigakari *began behind the performing platform and came directly towards the audience. This created an impression of distance; of characters coming from far away to enter the space of the action and the audience. Although the* hashigakari *now proceeds from the side to the stage rather than from behind to the stage, it is still set at the slight diagonal angle, so there is still a sense of coming forward to the 'place of action'.*

In contrast, the modern Kabuki stage is constructed as a proscenium theatre, but a wider version than the Western style. The audience is placed in front of the stage, with several levels of seating in the auditorium (stalls and balconies). When Kabuki began in the seventeenth century it originally used the same form as the square Noh platform stage, but with the raised walkway coming straight through the centre of the audience and joining the front of the stage. This bridge-walkway (in Kabuki, it is called the hanamichi), *still exists in modern Kabuki theatres but is now offset from the centre, joining the main stage nearer the wings on stage right. It travels from the very back of the auditorium and passes through the entire audience sitting in the stalls, and is raised to a height of about one metre, ensuring clear visibility for the actor. In this way actors can make their entrance from behind the audience and commence their performance, and their audience relationship, before they enter the main stage. L.M.*

Once the audience have found their place, they wait with anticipation; where will the actors come from? From stage right or stage left, or even from behind the audience? In Peter Brook's *Cherry Orchard*, Madame Ranevskaya and her friends came from behind the audience. They were coming from Moscow, which was distant and represented another way of life.

In Kabuki, stage right and the *hanamichi* represent the exterior world, so if the actor is supposed to be entering a house he always enters from this side, or from behind the audience.

Also in Kabuki Theatre, stage right is called the 'down' side, and stage left is the 'up' side, and modern Japanese theatre has continued to use the same terms. You can experiment; imagine someone is going to war, or to kill an enemy, and they hold a knife or gun in their hand. Let them walk from stage right to stage left, then do it the other way round (from stage left to stage right). Then ask the audience which one looks stronger. In my experience, from stage right to stage left looks stronger to most people. Then imagine that the character has finished the battle and goes home. Most people prefer the exit to go from stage left to stage right; it somehow gives the feeling of completion, as if something has finished. In Kabuki, you put important people on stage left, while lower people are placed stage right.

This stage-right-to-stage-left pattern reads as left-to-right from the audience point of view. The relative strength of this direction has also been observed in Western theatre, but has been attributed to the training of the audience's eye via reading. In the West we read from left to right, so that is how our eyes prefer to track. So the theory goes. But this is clearly not the case in Japanese theatre, since Japanese writing goes from right to left, beginning in what Westerners define as the 'back' of the book. Yet in theatrical terms the left-to-right pattern is still seen as more powerful. L.M.

In Kabuki the musicians are placed stage right and the storyteller is stage left. I was once told that the right brain is music and the left brain is language, but that you hear from the opposite ears; if you hear from the right ear it goes to the left brain and vice versa. Maybe this is why the Kabuki Theatre uses this arrangement. And I use this idea when I direct. For example, I placed the musician (Joao de Bruco) at stage right when I directed my production of a dance-theatre version of Jean Genet's *The Maids*. This is where his instruments were placed, which meant that from the audience perspective the music came more strongly to the left ear.

There is another factor I like to consider when making choices about entrances and exits. When important people enter I make them come from stage left, the 'high' side. In this same production of *The Maids*, most of the characters initially entered from stage right, the sole exception being Joao de Bruco. I have already mentioned that he was the musician, but in addition he fulfilled another function within the show. He was also the magician/storyteller who set events in motion. When he entered as the magician he was the most important character at that point of the play. So he came in from the 'high side' (stage left). When he was playing music he stayed at stage right for ear/brain reasons. The other 'high' character was the jailer/madame who always entered and exited from stage left.

Just as right and left are different in space, they are different in action. For example, turning to your right feels different from turning to your left. If you walk in small circles clockwise (to your right) you may feel your energy in one way, while if you walk anticlockwise you may feel it differently. Dervish turning is to the left (anticlockwise), operating as a way of calming down. The Nazi swastika is clockwise, while the virtually identical Buddhist symbol is anticlockwise.

In Japanese theatre, once you are on the stage there are a number of points with particular significance.

In the Noh Theatre there is a place called '*nanori*'. When you have left the *hashigakari* bridge you move to the centre of the stage and stop at the exact centre; this is *nanori*. It is the first place the main character stops, in order to explain who he is and why he is there, no matter which play he is in. *Nanori* means 'to present yourself' and the actor states the nature of his character ('I am a priest', or 'I am a god' et cetera) from this spot.

In the Kabuki Theatre a similar focal point exists. There is a place called *shichi-san*, which means 'seven-three', and it is the spot literally seven-tenths of the journey across the stage. Or there is *shiburoku*, which is 'four-six', which is nearer the middle. These are balanced visual points, where the audience can see the character and the harmony of the stage. In the same way there are two possible places to stop on the *hanamichi*.

For an actor the strongest position is facing the audience directly. Another strong position is the total back view. Usually, on the stage the strong angles are front, diagonal forty-five degrees (either right or left), then back, then side profile (again right or left). The back forty-five-degree angle is the weakest position on the stage. For the audience, even if the actor is not actually performing, the walk from upstage to downstage is very strong, like a close-up on camera. But if the actor goes from downstage to upstage it is like a fade-out. There is a sense of disappearing, even if your face is to the audience as you retreat to the back.

In many plays there is a conversation between two characters and for this the diagonals are useful, since they provide a sense of intimacy between the characters, while allowing the audience to see both actors' faces in three-quarter view. But in fact the strongest angle is both facing the public and this is often used in Kabuki.

When you speak your text, you work hard on the psychology, but if, while you are speaking, you change the angle of your body or the direction you are walking, you will also alter the audience's understanding. It is a different level of meaning.

When I act in a film, the director chooses how my body is seen by the audience. Whether a close-up, or torso, or face-on, or profile, or back view, the audience sees what the director has selected. But on the stage, actors can choose their own 'camera angle', influencing what the eye of the audience focuses on. They create the close-up or the wide shot. For example, if you want the audience to look at your face, you slowly lift it upwards and, when the face comes into full view, that will be their focus. Travelling from upstage to downstage is powerful in the same way. For example, if you walk from upstage to downstage it looks as if the camera is bringing you into clearer focus, zooming in on you. Of course, the audience for a live performance can always choose to look at something else (unlike film), but the actor has a surprising amount of influence on audience perception.

When I was performing in *The Mahabharata*, I played the role of Drona, a great master of the warrior arts. So I had to appear powerful and strong. Unfortunately I am quite small and I was surrounded by actors who were much taller than me, who were playing the parts of my students. I didn't want to appear as a small Japanese man surrounded by giants, so I employed a few tricks. In most scenes I kept a wide distance between myself and the others, so that the difference in height was less apparent. But when I had to be closer, I moved downstage of my partner, so that I was bigger from the audience point of view. There was another problem: at certain points I had to hug the other characters. What could I do in this case? During the hug, I went up on to tiptoe. I knew that the audience would focus on our faces at that point and whatever I did with my feet would pass unnoticed. I gained seven centimetres in height that way.

These little tricks are an actor's delight. In commercial theatre there are sometimes arguments between the lead actors about who is in front, who is seen better by the audience, who has the better angle. This is the unfortunate egoism of some actors.

CHARACTER

What is a character? From the audience point of view a character is a series of details – a way of walking, sitting, standing, gestures, turning the head, holding a cup; a sharpness in the voice, a softness in the hands – details which give you insight into the nature of that human being.

There is a well-known story. Once upon a time three blind men decided to discover an elephant. They went to the zoo and tried to find out what this animal called 'elephant' was like, since they had never encountered one in their lives before. Being blind, they had to use touch rather than sight in order to investigate. Each of them in turn touched the elephant, then they all came together again to discuss what they had encountered. The first man said, 'The elephant is like a snake. Long and thin. Twisting and turning as it moves.' The second man said, 'No, no, you're mistaken. It is a fan. It is flat and thin, and stirs the air as it waves back and forth.' The third man said, 'No, no, no! You've both got it all wrong! The elephant is like a round column, standing strong on the earth and going upwards towards the sky.' The three men kept arguing about their discoveries. They could not find any point of agreement and the discussion became heated, until finally they gave up. They went their separate ways, each convinced that he was right and the other two were either fools or liars.

In fact, all of them were correct. One man had touched the trunk, another had grasped the ear, while the third had felt the leg. None of them was wrong, but it is very hard to understand the entire truth. It is the same with character.

People say to me, 'You are kind', or 'You are cold', or 'You are wise', or 'You are stupid', or 'You are wicked', or 'You are impatient', or 'You are warm', or 'You are a charlatan', or 'You are honest', or 'You are a liar', or 'You are modest', or 'You are vain'. But I feel that all these judgements are imprecise. The question then arises 'Who am I?' and, truthfully, I have no answer. I really don't know who I am.

I enjoy going to performances of Bunraku, the traditional puppet theatre of Japan. In particular, I am always touched by stories involving romantic suicides.

Bunraku is the third classical theatre style in Japan. It was created during the same period as Kabuki, and the two theatre forms share many of their stylistic elements, such as music and external narration, and often use the same scripts. However, Bunraku employs puppets instead of human actors. The puppets are approximately one-third human size and require three skilled operators to manipulate them: a master operator and two assistants. The puppets' movements are extremely delicate and utilise similar gestural conventions as the human actors employ in the Kabuki. Stories of double suicides were very popular during the seventeenth century, and appear in both Kabuki and Bunraku. L.M.

I've watched many, many performances, always the same story, always exactly the same *mise-en-scène*. Yet every single time I am deeply moved by what I see. I ask myself why this happens when I see the puppet performance, while when the same story is told by Kabuki actors it does not touch me in the same way. When watching real actors, no matter how good they are, I am aware of something in the corner of their eye. Something that comes from the actors' self-consciousness, their fear, their need to be loved, their anguish. This is not a part of the character in the play. In Bunraku, because the face is only a puppet, this element from the actor is absent. As a result the performance has a certain purity. The acting simply tells the story.

Five hundred years ago in Japan there was a famous Zen Master called Ikkyu. One day he went to see the puppet theatre. During the performance he noted that the movement of the puppets was very interesting and amusing, and that the manipulator was handling a wide range of characters: a god, or a samurai, or a quiet modest lady. The manipulator did this so well that the puppets seemed to be alive. And the audience accepted that the stories they told were those of living, breathing human beings. When the puppet did something funny the audience laughed. When it became enraged the audience experienced its anger. And when it became sad and wept the audience also cried. And Ikkyu asked, 'Who are these creatures?' He discovered that they were made of an ordinary piece of wood. He then said that our own lives were the same. The creature moving about the stage looks like a real being, but only because the manipulator exists and is present behind the puppet.

He said that our existence is twofold: the physical life, which you can see, and a second existence deep inside all of us, which is invisible. If you insist only on your physical, visible existence, you start to believe that this is the reason for your life. Social life becomes your chief focus and you become very attached to the details of the physical world. This focus is a delusion. But equally, if you insist only on the invisible life you cannot function in society and your life becomes diminished. Ikkyu said that you must remain balanced in the middle of these two extremes.

Although Ikkyu is very famous in Japan, he did not fit the normal image of a saintly spiritual master. He lived during a period of great violence and turmoil. In his early years he lived in a Zen temple, but later chose to leave the temple and to live in the world, associating with thieves and beggars, and taking a lover. According to some, he degraded himself by choosing to associate with non-holy people, but for him it seemed false to remain in the purity (and wealth) of the temple, at such a difficult time. So he went into the world of robbers and desperate survival, in order to remain true to himself and reality.

The Japanese word for meditation is *Zazen* and this word is written with two pictograms: '*za*' and '*zen*'. The kanji for the first part ('*za*' meaning 'sitting') is made up in the following way: the symbol for 'human' is repeated twice, then placed above the symbol of 'the earth'. So the idea of 'sitting' is symbolised by two people sitting together and talking on the earth. In Zen, there are two versions of your 'self': your daily self, plus another self deep inside. Therefore, when you meditate, these two are sitting and having a conversation.

In Zen meditation the aim is to find your true being. Normally, we assume that this is the being we recognise from daily life. Our physical existence: eating, drinking, loving, becoming angry or happy or sad. Also your profession, your nationality, your race, your gender, even your name. All these things seem to make up 'who you are'. But according to Zen there is another 'true' self, which lies behind these elements: a kind of non-physical existence. You are normally unaware of this second 'self', so you have to work to discover it.

One day, at the beginning my career as an actor, I found myself alone and very sad. I cried. Tears fell down. Suddenly I wondered, 'What kind of face do I have?' So I went to the mirror and looked at my face. In real life I was sad and tearful. Yet on the other hand I had a professional curiosity about my appearance. So I asked myself, 'Who is this person who is curious?' I was a young man, who was weeping over the loss of a lover, but at the same time I was a young actor who wanted to see what kind of face he had at that moment of grief. In daily life there is 'a young man' and at the same time 'a young actor with curiosity'. Even at the very beginning I had the feeling that there were two people living in my body.

Ikkyu said that your physical existence and your non-physical existence need to be linked. You should not focus on one aspect or the other, but encourage an exchange between them. This enables you to be fully alive. On the stage it is the same thing: you act and at the same time you observe yourself acting. In addition, there is a flow between the observing and the acting. Eventually you forget about the observing and the doing. There is no conscious thought and you can be free. With that kind of freedom real life could also be wonderful.

YOURSELF AS A CHARACTER

When an actor plays Hamlet, he does not believe he loses his own identity and becomes an actual Danish prince called Hamlet. But neither does he think that all he needs to do is 'be himself', since that assumes that Hamlet is exactly the same as himself. Instead, he uses his own emotions or gestures as the same kind of gesture or emotion as Hamlet, to create an equivalent category of experience. In a role, you are never completely 'Hamlet', but neither are you your 'self'. You are living in the eye of the audience. You create an analogy of Hamlet, then make a connection between the two realities. The actor is always living in an odd situation.

In real life, when the waiter in the café is living his 'role' as waiter, it is the same as the actor playing Hamlet. He has created an analogy. But when you are playing Hamlet you know you are playing something that does not exist. You do not deceive yourself into believing that you really are Hamlet. But in daily life a person can really believe he is a 'waiter'.

Too often, people try to make themselves into one 'object', such as 'man' or 'French' or 'waiter'. We create a kind of sculpture of our 'self' and place this sculpture in the world. And the world in turn responds to it. Since we don't want to be destroyed by other people, we try to please the world. So the waiter tries to be a perfect waiter and if he succeeds, other people say 'He is a good waiter'. People struggle for a perfect realisation of their 'sculpture/analogy' in order to feel protected. But this is self-deception.

As I mentioned earlier, when I came to Europe I was playing the 'Japanese actor' and using Japanese technique. I wanted to feel secure, so I wanted to play the 'perfect Japanese actor'. It made me feel safe, inside that role. So when Peter said to me, 'Don't use your

Japanese technique any more,' I didn't wear kimono any longer, or use styles from Japanese theatre. I tried to avoid all my Japanese technique and inside I felt insecure. I didn't know who I was. I was very worried about myself. So I tried to throw away the self-deception and therefore the fear. Eventually, as I said, I did find a bit more freedom. But to be free is a terrible fear. It's easier to accept on the stage because you know you are not really Hamlet; there is no self-deception. Hamlet doesn't exist, except when the actor plays the part. When the play ends there is nothing left; not Hamlet, nor the fantasy. In daily life it is different. The play never ends until you die, so you want to live that self-deception right to the end. But that is not freedom.

In real life my character isn't one single thing. Sometimes it is heavy, sometimes light. That is true of anyone's character: many aspects, never one single thing. But when I am talking about my character like this it is because I am watching myself. So who is watching that character? I am sure that inside me there is someone who is watching. We already know that it is useful to look at what we are feeling, and what we are doing, and why we make certain choices. In fact, we always look at these things. But it is also very important to find out who is doing the looking. When we look at all the details of our daily life somebody is watching. There is an observer. This is the same relationship that exists between the actor and the character.

You are angry, or crying, or you are worried or afraid, and it is really happening on the stage, completely, in the character. At the same time you are also coolly watching that person raging or crying or trembling in fear. This means that two things are occurring simultaneously on the stage, leading to a very balanced state. As the character you are totally immersed in the fear or anger, while as an actor you are very cool and calm.

I wish I could find a way to maintain the same point of view in real life: to feel everything, but at the same time not get involved in my emotions. In addition, when I am acting I pay careful attention to what people say; I look inside them to see who they really are; I respond with awareness and sensitivity; I feel the right timing to do an action or say a phrase. It makes good acting, but in fact this is how I should respond all the time. I am sure my relations with other people would be better if I did.

People often say that my movements seem very careful and precise, but that is only true when I perform. In daily life I am very clumsy: always falling down, knocking over the wine, bumping into things. In real life I don't act the way I do on stage and I am always asking myself why I don't use my stage approach in daily life. I would like to be able to live my normal life with the same attention I use on the stage. In fact, I believe acting provides very good practice for daily life.

I have been acting for more than fifty years, but I cannot always apply what I have learned to my daily existence. This is why I have to keep working.

CONTRADICTION

I have a lot of memories associated with Shakespeare's play *The Tempest*. When I first worked with Peter, it was on a version of *The Tempest* (at the Roundhouse theatre in London in 1968). I played Ariel, a spirit of the air. I was told he was always jumping around and flying, but I decided I would never attempt to jump or fly, but that my feet should remain on the ground all the time: the complete opposite.

At the beginning of the seventies meditation was very fashionable in Europe. Around this time I met a Master of yoga, who looked very serious and had the appearance of a 'True Master'. But I know that in Asia real masters do not look like that. At first glance a real master looks like a charlatan. The first impression of this man was of a 'Great Master' and so I was sure that he was a charlatan.

In real life, before you meet somebody, his or her reputation sets up a picture in your mind. But in many cases, when you actually meet the person you discover the complete opposite to what you expected. So when I play a character, at first I try the total opposite. However, I must be careful. If the only thing I do is to focus on doing the opposite, it just becomes a game or a joke. At first I try to taste that opposite, while linking to the story, and little by little I digest it inside. I sense how this contradiction links to the words I say and the relations around me. I am not looking to be original or creative; that is just a false game. Instead, I have to discover the unexpected elements, but at the same time find out what is true. When I construct my character, if I think at a certain moment that I should shout the words, I try instead to do the text while laughing. People are complex and unexpected.

Many years after the Roundhouse *Tempest* I played Gonzalo in Peter's later version of the play. He was described as a kind and wise man, so I decided never to play him as wise. Instead, I tried to make him a bit funny and stupid, and without any appearance of kindness. In this way, the audience first sees something contradictory, but gradually as the play goes on, they understand that Gonzalo is a kind man. You start with the opposite, but because you have to speak the lines of Shakespeare, and do the actions of Gonzalo, little by little the kindness of Gonzalo appears.

Even if you are playing a man who looks stupid but is actually wise, you have to give something that is convincing to the audience. If you play the appearance of a wise man, in a way it will work; the audience will say to themselves, 'Oh, he is a wise man.' But when the information is given to the audience in too clear a way they switch off. If he looks stupid, yet there is a question that maybe he is wise, the audience will be interested in understanding the real personality. There is a space for their imagination. The audience works as well as the actors.

As I said above, when our logical analysis of the character suggests that at a given point he or she should be thinking 'anger', try the opposite. Try smiling. It is the same thing with movement: if you think you should go to the right, try going to the left. Or, as you approach your partner, if you feel you need to go close to him, instead go back. Or you may decide you want to say a piece of text with your head down at a certain moment. Try doing it with your head lifted. By exploring the opposite, you may discover something better that your first logical idea.

But below the surface of the character there is yet another level: the energy of the actor. If this is strong, the public begins to sense something special. They can see that the character you are playing is a truly horrible person, yet at the same time they can appreciate the actor's special quality. Good acting occurs when the audience hates the nasty man, but at the same time, on the deep human level, the public can be deeply moved by seeing the actor making that character live. They hate the villain on the stage, but they have a different relationship with the actor who plays the role. They can sense that the being of the actor is beautiful, so they love him while at the same time hating the character.

This is not an intellectual understanding of the character's inner-most turmoil, not even an empathy for the character's situation, but a deeper empathy with the actor himself. It is like a meeting of two people: the actor and the public through the character. So you can have a special kind of relation. In daily life you rarely meet people on this deep level, but on the stage you can see both the villainous character and the generous actor. Therefore you can have a very deep human relationship with the actor via the character.

After the performance your body is dead as that character. Your consciousness has manipulated that character on the stage, but when you finish your consciousness lets the character go. Then you go home and play the character of the husband, or the father, but your consciousness is still something separate. Consciousness has no name, no colour, no form. But we all have it and you can apply it to your daily life.

As an actor on stage, getting lost in the character is not a useful objective. When you get drunk you lose your daily attitude; you go somewhere else where you can get rid of many psychological problems. The same thing can happen in acting. But this is not a controlled state. It is almost a state of unconsciousness, like the effects of a drug or a trance. When actors say 'I was completely lost in the character' or 'I don't have any memory of what I was doing', this is not good acting. Instead, we should try to watch the character and what is happening, instead of being unaware. But if you watch too much, your body disengages and nothing happens. This is too much the other way. As I said earlier, developing *ri-ken-no-ken* can help with this problem.

THOUGHT AND TEXT

Once, when I was teaching a workshop, I asked the participants what they concentrated on when they were acting. They replied, 'Situation and emotion.' Later I asked Peter what he thought about this and he said, 'Yes, the situation is very important. Where you are and what you are doing affect you very much. They change you. Concentrating on the precise thoughts moment by moment is also very important, since these will enable emotion to appear naturally. But if you think about emotion you become the prisoner of thought about emotion. You lose freedom.' In fact, when actors perform, emotion will be born naturally. If we try to fix it in advance we do lose freedom. What is important is situation and thought, not emotion.

When you act, it isn't just describing the dramatic situation with words. We already know that if you take the precise body position, the corresponding emotion will come. Body and emotion are linked, and words can be the trigger for these deeper connections. If you place your body in a neutral position, then say 'I am angry', some-how that language will transform your body. The emotion will come because words seem to be some form of magic, like an incantation. If I say the words 'I am calm', calmness will come.

A key phrase here is, 'The body is neutral.' Before this 'word-magic' can work, the actor must have a neutral body. If the body is already contorted with rage and the actor says 'I am calm', it is unlikely to work. Only an open body can receive the suggestion of the word and allow the language to affect the inner life. L.M.

When you are at the swimming pool and you dive from the springboard, the flexibility of the wood allows you to go higher. The word is a kind of springboard that allows you to go to another state.

In addition, when we are acting we are very often speaking a text that is describing something, or imagining something, or hoping for something. In this case it is useful to visualise the scene in the mind and then describe what we actually see, using the words. The actor must not perceive the words of the text as they are written down in the script, but instead should see the scene as a visual reality.

I am very bad with foreign languages, and I have many problems learning and speaking them, and I always retain a definite Japanese accent. Unfortunately, most of my performances in recent years have been in either French or English, which are not comfortable for me. When rehearsals begin, I normally tend to visualise the lines of the written text in the third eye, then read that text when I speak, like an autocue. But it feels clumsy. So I try to make the words sound more normal. To do this, I follow the visual path and try to see the image of what I am describing, like a film. When I do this the text flows more easily and the nuances seem natural. Unfortunately, my pronunciation is still bad.

A good source of speeches that include a strong visual element can be found in all the plays from Greek tragedy. In each play there is a scene where a messenger enters and describes events that he or she has witnessed, away from the stage. These are pivotal scenes, often describing the death of a major character, and they describe the events in precise and vivid detail. L.M.

USING THE MAP

During the rehearsals the itinerary or map for the play has been created; the text has been learned and you have explored the thoughts and the character. In addition, decisions have been made about the space and how to use it. But this is only a beginning. The actor still has to focus on how actually to use this blueprint on the night of performance. The journey has been mapped in great detail, but how do we actually get from A to B to C on a moment-by-moment basis?

I begin at the beginning. At the start of any theatrical performance the audience isn't really ready to go into the show. The actors have to consider how to enable the audience to enter the performance. Like driving a car, you start with first gear. At that moment you need a lot of petrol. When it is running at the proper speed you can ease off.

Peter always works a lot on the first part of the production. He said that once the show starts you can go with it. It fact, it is difficult to start a show for both the actors and the audience, and you must work to get it right. One actor from the modern theatre in Japan began a show with an entrance where he had to appear from inside a house and come down a staircase. He rehearsed that entrance for one week.

In his book *The Threads of Time*, Peter describes the first scene in the play *The Man Who*:

Yoshi Oida came to the table, lit the candle with a special concentration, and then for a long time gazed intently at the flame. Then he blew it out, took another match, lit the candle, and blew it out again. As he started once more, I could feel the tension in the audience increasing. The audience could read into the simple actions far more than they apparently expressed; for this, the audience needed no preparation, no education, no reference, and above all no culture. It understood directly what was going on. We seemed at last to be approaching the transparency that for so long had been our aim.

I read this and felt it was a great honour to be praised in this way, but in fact, when I am acting I have no idea whether it is good or bad. Sometimes, when I think about everything and I am happy with my work, people say it isn't good. In a way, actors never really know. We always want to be good, but sometimes people say 'good', sometimes 'bad', so it is very hard for the actor to judge. I am happy working with Peter because I can trust his judgement, but as an actor I wonder what were the elements that produced this positive reaction. I want to analyse why it worked.

I know that during this scene I was not consciously using my theatre skills, or employing the actor's techniques for playing a character. Nevertheless, I was aware that the audience was responding well and seemed to be engaged. In general, actors try to tell a story and the audience listens. But for me the aim was different; I wanted to share the mysteries of the brain with the audience. I wasn't trying to play the scene well, or to create 'good theatre', or to entertain the audience.

I began by walking towards the candle and sitting in a chair facing it. During this action I wanted the audience to focus on my physical state and to bring their attention to the movements of my body. My attitude was nothing to do with the attitudes of ordinary life; I had to find the exact image of someone with brain damage. For this, the observations the actors had done in the hospital were very useful. My character had a particular neurological problem: when he saw objects (in this case candle and match), he could not resist making a connection and using those objects. So he immediately used the match to light the candle. At that moment, while I was doing this action I had almost no consciousness of who I was and what the audience was thinking about my character. I simply concentrated on the match and the matchbox in order to make fire.

Next, I wanted the audience to focus their gaze on my hands and on the matches that were placed beside the candle. Only the matches and my hands, nothing else. I picked up a match as if it were a little stick, and fixed my attention on the moment for lighting it. I couldn't rush it, or wait too long. It had to be exactly the right moment. This wasn't a matter of counting but of instinct. Not only my own instinct; I had to sense the moment when the audience felt I should light the candle. It was essential that it be lit precisely when the audience wanted me to do it.

The next problem was to know when to blow it out. Again, not too soon or too late – the right moment. And once more it was the audience who gave me the signal every night (though they were not aware of this responsibility). Then I had to repeat the action: light the candle and extinguish it. Obviously, I couldn't just repeat what I had done the first time. The tempo had to be faster than the previous sequence and the position of my body needed to be slightly different. It was a very precise moment; in that space there were only four elements: the brain-damaged man, the match, the audience and me, nothing else.

The movement for lighting the match originated in the arm. In fact, my aim was not to strike the match, but to move the arm correctly. And as for the arm movement itself, it came from what can be described as 'the harmony of the body'. In fact, it was this general state that enabled me to move my arm organically, which resulted in the candle being correctly lit.

Even though the beginning of the play requires care, attention and energy, it is equally important not to push too hard.

One of Buddha's students was working very seriously on his spiritual training, but he wasn't advancing at all. Buddha came to him and said, 'I heard that when you lived at home you were a very good player of the harp. Is that true?' The student answered, 'Yes, I did play very well.' Buddha went on, 'When you played, what happened if the strings were too tight?' 'The sound wasn't very good.' 'And if they were loose?' 'If they were too loose the sound was also bad.' 'So what did you do to the strings in order to create a good sound?' The student replied, 'Neither too tight nor too loose, but tuned correctly to give the right pitch.' Buddha said, 'Our training is the same thing. If you work with too much effort your heart becomes too frantic. You cannot find calm. But if you don't use enough effort it becomes boring and unproductive.'

I am a very bad cook. Whenever I am cooking I start to think, 'Maybe there isn't enough salt,' so I add more and it ends up too salty. Or: 'It isn't cooked enough,' so I keep it on the stove longer and it ends up overcooked or burnt. I don't trust the cooking materials and I feel I need to do something extra to make it better. As a result it is always too much, or overdone. It never works. Acting is the same. When you perform you always feel it isn't enough, so you push. Then the audience has too much information and the performance is no longer interesting. You do it very well, but it's boring to watch. You simply need to trust the material that you have.

INNER SPACE

According to Buddhist teaching the heart is like a monkey who jumps from branch to branch: always moving about, never being quiet and calm. It is trembling, quaking and shaking, uncontrolled and unpredictable. Quieting the heart isn't easy. One thing that can help is the Buddhist practice of *sanmai*.

In *An Actor Adrift* I mentioned that in the Zen monastery there were three important concepts used for meditation: *tanden-riki*, *sanmai* and *kufu*. *Tanden-riki* is placing your energy in the *tanden* point. This prevents your meditation becoming weak or empty. *Kufu* refers to the tricks or techniques involved in maintaining concentration, such as counting your breaths or focusing on an image. *Sanmai* is the awareness of each moment and the focus on the simple activity of that moment: when you eat you simply think about eating; when you walk, just concentrate on walking – one thing only.

The actor's job is *sanmai*. At each moment you focus on how to speak that line, how to make that single gesture and how to concentrate on the immediate emotional reaction. This is the theory, but somehow I always find myself thinking, 'Oh, I didn't do that very well,' or, 'What is the next line?' Sometimes you hear coughs from the audience and you get annoyed and say to yourself, 'Why is he disturbing this wonderful moment?' At other times I wonder what the audience is thinking when I am standing there at a particular point. I find myself saying, 'Maybe I should change the way I stand,' or, 'Why is my stage partner so bad?' These extra thoughts come, but they don't help at all.

On the stage you try to reproduce details of the activity very carefully. When you speak to other actors, you try to listen attentively. You concentrate fully on trying to understand what other people are saying, in order to create a good quality of relationship. Your actions are the same thing. Each detail of the movement is concentrated. When you pick up the teapot you are aware of your action. You pick up the cup with care. And you can do this if you bring your attention to the moment. Occasionally actors are clumsy, and our mind slips in and out, but at least you are trying to do it.

When I was younger I studied the tea ceremony in Japan. One day the Master asked me to make tea for him. Although I was nervous, I started by following the precise form of the tea ceremony ritual. I focused on the exact details of what I had to do: how to touch the cup; listen to the water boiling; carefully take water; put green tea powder into the bowl; carefully touch the napkin; carefully mix the hot water with the tea powder. Finally I completed the whole process of the tea ceremony and placed the cup of tea in front of my tea Master. He said, 'Yes, I feel you have made delicious tea.' Then he took his first sip.

But when I was doing the ceremony I wasn't thinking about making wonderful tea. I was simply concentrating on the process. The master who was watching saw my activity in a different light; he built up in his imagination the taste of the tea. Even before tasting the tea, he had drawn his own conclusion.

The same thing happened to me. Once I was watching the ceremonial preparation of a carp. The Shinto priest was cutting the fish in a very ritual way. After the ceremony the fish was grilled and offered to the onlookers. When I tasted that fish it seemed so delicious. I don't know if it was truly superior to any other fish, or whether, simply through watching the ceremony, my imagination created this impression.

CONCENTRATION AND IMAGINATION

In Peter Brook's book *The Threads of Time* he describes a particular improvisation we did in the early days of the group:

> In the beginning we allowed no-one to observe our experiments – and yet we needed spectators. If we were only to be watched by ourselves, we would quickly fall into the narcissism we wished to avoid. However, our experiments were too fragile to bear the blows of harsh criticism. So the first to be invited into our space were children, and they taught us a lot, because their reactions were immediate and penetrating. Initially, we tried to encourage the children to enjoy the freedom of the space, but to our dismay they just ran wild. After a humiliating session when they had seized our bamboo sticks, chased us into corners, and beat us up, we thought again. We had seen the way a false freedom leads to chaos and realised there was no point in giving children an experience that was no different from running and screaming in their own playground. We could not be casual; they deserved something better, and this compelled us to study the precise conditions that govern focus and concentration. At the next session we began differently. Very quietly, we assembled the children round a platform, and the

actors, using very simple improvisations, such as exploring the mysterious and comic possibilities of a cardboard box, had no difficulty in holding their attention and their imagination. Then the actors attempted a very difficult experiment, which was to come down from the platform and walk among the children in order to see if they were still capable of maintaining the same silence and concentration without staying at a point of command. Naturally, once the dominant position was lost, the children's attention went with it. (p. 151)

Peter then wrote that I had managed to his surprise to restore the lost concentration. I asked myself how this had come about and realised that for me the perspective was different. The actual improvisation was about a fisherman who had saved the life of a turtle. In gratitude, the turtle invited the fisherman to visit his palace in the depths of the ocean. The first scene was played on a platform one metre by two metres square, and the descent into the ocean demanded that I step off the platform and move among the children. Normally, in a children's show, when actors walk among the spectators the children touch their bodies or talk to them. I needed a lot of courage for that moment of stepping off the platform, since I didn't want the children's reactions to break the atmosphere of being at the bottom of the sea. To keep the children at a distance and to prevent them touching me as if I were a friend passing through, I had to erect invisible barriers, somehow to retain an exterior relationship with this particular audience. I tried to make a kind of emptiness, so that when I walked among the children they would stay silent and engaged, and that this would remain, even when I disappeared briefly from sight.

At the moment when I was going from the 'boat' into the 'water', I was concentrating on joining my world with the world of the children – not thinking about how to move or act, but only about how to make this happen. I had to erect an invisible barrier and I asked myself how I could do this. Normally, actors work through finding a character or an emotion, but that approach wasn't relevant here. Without thinking about character or emotion, I simply imagined that I was in the water and that I was walking through it, while the children were the fish swimming about. I was hoping that my imagination would create a useful concentration in myself and my body activity, and that this would somehow make a barrier between me and the children. I was strongly concentrated on this image in my imagination and totally engaged with the situation.

Sometimes in real life, when you watch football and a player is about to kick for goal, everybody is united in a strong wish that the ball should go into the net. All their concentration is wish and will. In a café there is a beautiful woman and with my concentration I will her to look at me. Turn your head towards me, please, turn your head. That is my very strong wish. Sometimes it works, sometimes it doesn't. This is the same as when I am playing: there is a very strong wish that the audience stays interested in my actions. It is exact: look at this pen; or even look at this end of this pen. When I was working with the children my aim was to enclose them within a big circle, a totality. And with the candle in *The Man Who*, it was simply to get them to see the match and the matchbox, to see the flame, to see the candle, and to see the relation between the candle and my eye.

ENERGY

There is an old Japanese story. A big rat entered a house and took over a room. This rat was very strong and fierce. The owner of the house became angry and disturbed, since the rat was constantly breaking things, biting people and generally creating a mess. So the owner put his cat into the room. But the rat attacked the cat, who immediately ran away. The owner then asked his neighbours to loan him their strongest, toughest cats, and one by one he introduced these animals into the rat's room. But every single one of these cats was bitten to pieces by the rat and ran away. Finally, the owner grabbed a stick and decided to deal with the rat himself. The man rushed around the room, flailing at the rat (who was as fast as he was strong). Every time he hit out at the rat, the rat dodged and escaped, and the man achieved nothing, except breaking even more of the furniture. Then the rat jumped up and bit the man on his face. Just as he was about to give up, the man heard about a famous, super-strong cat and arranged for it to be brought to his house. When he saw the cat he was shocked; it was old, the body was flabby and lacking energy. Even though the cat looked totally unreliable, he decided to trust its reputation and see if it could deal with the rat. He put the cat into the room and immediately the rat went rigid. He was totally immobilised. The cat strolled up to the rat, gently picked him up in his mouth and carried him out of the room.

All the neighbourhood cats were intrigued by this cat's power and invited him to explain what he did. They asked 'What kind of technique did you use?', 'How did you do it?', then they asked the cat to teach them. The old cat asked each of them in turn to describe the techniques they had attempted to use. The first cat said, 'My technique involves jumping high, or squeezing through tiny spaces. I use quick, acrobatic-style movements, so even if the rat had gone up to the ceiling I could have caught it. This technique has always worked before.' The old cat replied, 'You have learned the correct movements of the body, but when you use only outside movement you cannot defeat your enemy.'

A second cat spoke up: 'To catch the rat requires concentration of internal energy, using the power of *ki*. I have studied how to develop my internal energy and how to make it extremely strong. In this way, when I see the enemy I simply show them my internal energy, and they are terrified at the sight of such power. Thus I can defeat my enemies. Until now.' The old cat answered, 'If you depend on that internal energy and you show your intention to kill your enemy, the enemy can use the same internal power to resist you. And if that other person's internal power is stronger than yours, your internal power is of no use.'

The third cat said, 'I tried to use my inner energy to evoke harmony with the other and, through this harmony, to discover how to defeat my enemy. If someone else has a strong internal energy, I don't try to resist at all.' The old cat replied, 'What you call harmony is not real harmony. It is artificial and consciously constructed. If you have this kind of conscious, manufactured "harmony", it destroys your free movement.'

The old cat continued, 'Physical technique is important, internal energy is important and harmony is important. But beyond that is the free mind. Like water it can travel anywhere. It is a natural empty state of "no mind". If you enter this, your technique, your internal energy, your harmony can work effectively. If you are only there, being truly there, the rat disappears, and there is no need to fight with the rat; he is gone. To defeat your enemy, you have no consciousness of yourself. Nor do you have consciousness of the object called "rat".

'But even that state is not a perfect state. True unconsciousness is not just about making the mind empty. You have no consciousness of the fact that your mind is empty. You are not caught by the conception of "emptiness". You simply react to the world around you.'

I wrote in *An Actor Adrift* that I had once asked my Noh teacher when an actor might expect to find freedom in performance. Since the master of the school has the responsibility of maintaining 600 years of tradition, he has to be very strict. Master Yataro Okura said that you work hard until you are sixty years old, then after that age you can be free for the first time. But even so, since you have been training for sixty years, you don't go too far from the classic form. When he reached the age of eighty I reminded him that a long time ago he had said that after sixty it was possible to be free. So I asked him whether he felt free after that age. He said, 'No, what I said was wrong. Only genius actors can be free. Myself, on the stage, I was not free at all, since I was concentrating on not making a mistake about the choreography, nor forgetting the text. Because of my age, I was preoccupied with remembering everything correctly. I was not free at all. Only geniuses can be free.' I met him again when he was ninety-five. At that point he said, 'I have forgotten everything a classical actor should do.'

In the Noh style of theatre, every detail of the action is fixed by tradition and learned by imitation. There is no improvisation, or space for personal interpretation of character. No actor is permitted to deviate from a learned formula, unless permitted by the Head of the School. What Yoshi calls 'freedom' is more a matter of internal connection than external experiment. L.M.

TIMING

The main target of all acting is to create life on stage.

But what is 'life'? In fact, 'life' is always changing, it never stays the same for very long. Unfortunately, actors often look for unchanging states when performing. They look for a single strong emotion, or an idea, or a level of intensity. But this isn't true to life. Life is constantly changing, and our feelings and reactions do the same thing. Actors must be aware of the need to shift. This can involve shape, or tempo and, if working with text, pitch and rhythm. Emotion is also an element that you can use to manifest change. But in addition actors have to sense when and how to shift. And this is a question of timing.

When I was a young man I sometimes acted in Kyogen performances. Once, I performed the role of a seaweed seller, who had to sing a song asking people to buy his seaweed. After the performance a great Master, Yagoro Okura (who was the father of my own teacher and had been in the audience) said, 'The last phrase of the song should be longer than what you did. Try to sing it again.'

So, in my dressing room, I had to sing the same song for him. And I elongated the final vowel as he had instructed. Then I discovered that 'Oh yes! I really, really want to sell my seaweed!' Just a five-second prolongation of the vowel, and I felt that I truly wanted to sell, and the song itself appeared more full of the need to convince people to buy.

As I mentioned earlier, I met the French dancer Jean Babilée a few years back. Babilée is old, so he cannot move as much as he did fifty years ago, but when I watched him perform, I could see that he is still a very good dancer. His movements were small, but his timing was fantastic and his moments of stillness had great power. Everything seemed to happen at exactly the right moment, in exactly the right way.

Actors need to be aware of changing and transforming each moment in an organic way. If someone says 'Oh, the scene went on too long!' or 'It is too short', this is a problem of the actor's timing; if he can find the right variety and make the changes in an organic way, the audience will not notice these things.

BREATH AND TIMING

In *The Invisible Actor* I talked about the importance of breath. Breathing is a very powerful physical process and, according to your breath pattern, you feel different inside. In fact, you are changed.

Naturally, when you alter your breathing in this way the impression the audience receives is also different. But this isn't simply a matter of the audience visually registering a physical change in the performer. They actually breathe along with the actor. And because they are breathing with you, they are also physically changed by your breath. For example, when you stop breathing in a performance you create a certain tension for yourself, and for the audience. So if you have a moment of great drama, stop breathing and the audience will do the same.

When I was young, I studied the *Gidaiyu* tradition of storytelling, which is used in the theatres of both Kabuki and Bunraku. The scripts are fixed and so are the pauses. When I was practising in front of my teacher, Jyuzo Tsuruzawa, I just breathed in normally during the pause. He immediately stopped me, saying, 'Here is a moment of tension. If you breathe in normally at this point, you will lose all the drama of that scene. So when you pause at that moment, stop breathing, then quickly take in air just before you recommence speaking.' He gave me other useful advice. 'When you are speaking a long phrase and you run out of breath in the middle, don't actively try to take in more air. Just open your mouth and the air will flow in by itself. There is a difference between consciously breathing in and just letting the mouth open.'

IMPROVISED PERFORMANCE

Until now I have been discussing the elements involved in creating a map through the rehearsal process, then the use of this map in actual performance. But what happens when you decide not to use a clearly defined itinerary?

In 1979, when we were preparing the production of *The Conference of the Birds* for the Festival of Avignon, Peter asked the actors to make their own one-person show. For a long time I had wanted to make a performance using the Chinese text of the Zen *Koan*.

A Koan is a paradoxical question used in Zen Buddhist teaching. They are used as tools for waking the mind of the student, and are questions that have no logical answer. A well-known Koan is 'What is the sound of one hand clapping?' Through wrestling with these paradoxes, a student's understanding may break through to a higher level. L.M.

In a sense, the Koan questions are like Beckett or Ionesco; an anti-theatre text. When you follow the text, you can't understand the meaning; but behind the text there is another level. So the text of *Interrogations* is just question and answer, but this is only the outside. A deeper level of question and answer is hiding behind the words, and this is interesting to investigate via theatre. So I asked the audience various questions. They weren't easy to answer; in five minutes you cannot find the answer. After all, in the Zen monastery you might spend three or four years looking for an answer. It was simply the starting point for the show and the aim was to make a theatrical relationship.

In using this text, the main question was how can I make a human relationship between the audience and myself? So with music (there was also a musician improvising during the show) and my movement I tried to create some kind of relationship. Certain elements were fixed; I told specific stories and asked particular questions. But beyond that it was open; audience members could provide their own replies or comments. In this case I had to respond immediately and spontaneously. My movements were improvised and so was the music. It was seventy minutes of performance, but the fixed text was less than ten minutes. I used certain elements in every performance, such as bamboo sticks, so some physical moments went in a similar direction every night, but nothing was choreographed.

When I was creating *Interrogations*, I wanted to learn how to improvise with dance, since this was a skill I had never learned. I went first to American choreographer Carolyn Carlson. She said that improvisation had three elements: direction, shape of the body and tempo. The second teacher I visited was the Japanese dancer Hideyuki Yano. He said that you should create a map on the stage: pathways and journeys. And that while you travel along those pathways you discover your body movement. The third artist I visited was Kazuo Ohno, the co-founder of Butoh. He said, 'I can't tell you how to move.' Instead, he gave me many images. According to the image you move. For example, he said, 'You are a skeleton, with no muscles at all.' While I was improvising with that image he said,

'Don't do too much. Don't try physically to imitate the skeleton. Do less. Simply.'

After we finished working he made some instant noodles for me.

I have been touring this show since 1979, performing in many different countries. This is a long time to keep the same show in repertoire. Most shows become old-fashioned or worn out. But because *Interrogations* was never fixed, I could always invent material and responses for the audience. This helped to keep it alive and contemporary. What is interesting for me is the question of tempo and timing; every day I had to build it up from zero. Sometimes I would sense that I was spending too long talking to the audience, so suddenly I had to speed things up. Or, how long should I stay with the audience before going on to the next story? Every time I had to judge this timing for myself.

Interrogations was a production with a semi-fixed itinerary. But it is possible to work with an even freer model. No map at all. The shows Brook's company performed in Africa were in this style. We began with a single idea such as 'a boot', or 'walking', and let the show develop from there. Actors could enter and leave the performing area when they wished, and could take the action in any direction they chose. When we began our journey, we tried to use a show we had prepared in Paris. But in the various African villages it fell completely flat. We thought that this show would work just as well in Africa as it had in the studio in Paris. But, of course, it didn't. So we decided to try another way. We resolved to make a show that was completely invented in front of the audiences and in the process discovered it is actually very difficult to create spontaneously in this way.

One day Andreas Katsulas, an American actor, decided to place a boot on the carpet. Suddenly the audience became very interested; the boot fascinated them. This is something I understand very well as a Japanese person, because in the past we only had sandals. Then when Japan became Westernised we started to import shoes, but they were very expensive. So a leather boot was a symbol of wealth, high class and success – a very interesting object. We improvised with that boot in front of that audience. One actor put on the boots and was transformed into a powerful personality. Another actor put on the boots and became a beautiful lady, but as soon as the boots were removed the transformation vanished. The boots also changed into other objects such as musical instruments.

What I learned through these shows was that it is possible to make a performance based on free improvisation. But you need a strong theme that is simple and can be grasped immediately by everyone. You also need a lot of imagination, and the ability to be quick and spontaneous. The show is less like a normal theatrical performance and more like a football game. The players must pay very close attention to what the rest of the team are doing and be ready to catch the ball at any time. In this way it was possible to develop the stories, without needing points of security. If it goes well, it can be more alive and exciting than a show that is fixed and unchanging. It looks like a concert of very good jazz improvisers. But it is very hard to do and you cannot guarantee the same quality every night.

In fact, when you perform in any theatre production there is always an element of improvisation. Sometimes it is totally free; the actor can move anywhere he or she chooses as the action unfolds. Or when the *mise-en-scène* is fixed, the actor must remain free internally. Every night is a unique relationship with that particular audience, and the actor must find a way to keep the communication alive and responsive.

When people ask me about the difference between acting in films and on the stage, I always answer that in films I feel that the director is the cook. The actors simply provide the raw materials for the cookery. The director chooses where to cut the film, arranges the tempo and so on. But in the theatre the actor has more responsibility. The elements of timing, rhythm, volume and energy all depend on the actors. And since every night the audience is different, every night the actor has to sense exactly what is needed. We have a lot of responsibility and we are always improvising.

When I was a beginner, one of my directors took me aside and said, 'You must realise, Yoshi, that you are not a genius.' Although I was disappointed, I understand that what he said was true. Only when the God of Theatre comes down can I approach genius. The rest of the time I just do my best for the audience. The relationship between actor and audience is similar to that between bus driver and passengers. I put the audience into the bus, and drive them to another time and space. The aim is to bring them to this time and space, not to show them what I can do.

6   After the Show

At the end of a performance the audience wants to move; after all, they have been sitting still for two hours or more. They also want to give the actors something, so they clap their hands. I believe this is very healthy – for the audience. Clapping hands stimulates the acupuncture points on the hand. But as an actor I prefer to receive silence after a show . . . then . . . after a while . . . wild applause.

People often come back to my dressing room after the performance and say things like 'I enjoyed the show very much' or 'It was wonderful'. Obviously, I like the applause (whenever it occurs), and I am very happy that they came and enjoyed themselves. At the same time I am aware that the compliments also belong to the director, and the technicians, and the writer. So I am enjoying the pleasure of compliments that actually should be shared with other people. On the other hand I am also aware that only the people who liked the show come back and offer these comments; the ones who disliked it or were bored won't be there. It is very important to remember that not everyone likes the performance. Maybe the majority of the audience didn't like it, but at least one or two individuals enjoyed it and took the trouble to tell me. That makes me happy.

During the run of Peter Brook's production of *The Tempest* they said the usual things like 'It was a very good show' or 'It was very entertaining and amusing'. The word that appeared most often was 'enjoyed'. One day Peter made a request of the actors. While we were backstage, instead of talking, he asked us to keep silent. We followed that direction and after the show the people who came backstage said something different. They said, 'We were moved.' This is a very different word. Something had changed through us remaining silent. Something happened that was not logical. The silence led to the comment 'moved'. But when we were chattering backstage, the audience's comment was 'enjoyed'. What was the difference between 'enjoyed' and 'moved'? It was the same text, the same *mise-en-scène*. Of course, a few days later we started talking backstage again and the audience response also returned to 'enjoy'; they no longer said that they had been 'moved'.

After I leave my dressing room I go to the café for a drink. Even here people sometimes come up to pay me compliments. I feel it is nice that they enjoyed watching the character in the play. The character was crying, or yelling, or feeling extremes of love and hate, but this wasn't real; it was something performed by the actor Yoshi Oida. Then I suddenly realise that even here, in the café, I am still playing a character: an actor called 'Yoshi Oida'. I try to make this character interesting by adding decoration and detail: 'kind', 'amusing', 'charming', 'interesting', 'humorous', 'gentle', 'teasing'.

Then I go home and start getting ready for bed. I take off my clothes and leave behind the responsibility of playing any kind of character. As I brush my teeth, I look into the bathroom mirror. I see a face, which has the attributes of 'man', 'old', 'Japanese'. Suddenly I have another question: is this face in the mirror my real 'self', or is it yet again another character? Is there somebody else behind him?

On the stage the curtain has gone down on my character, yet Yoshi Oida still exists. But what will happen when the curtain goes down on Yoshi Oida? I don't know.

When Ikkyu died, a student asked Ikkyu's companion, 'What is death?' She replied that it is 'someone in a hurry to go further'.

Appendix

TEACHING AND LEARNING
by Lorna Marshall

Several years ago Yoshi and I were sitting in a café, chatting about teaching and training methods. He suddenly turned to me and said, 'You know, in my teaching there aren't any new or special exercises. What matters is *how* you do them. And one thing that is very important is the timing of the exercises. If the exercises are too long, or too short, or in the wrong order, it doesn't work.' And he had hit the nail on the head.

When most of us think about the training process we tend to ask, 'If I do (or teach) this exercise, what will be learned?' We work on the assumption that an exercise is *about* a specific skill or concept, and that if we do that exercise, that skill or concept will be transferred to us – a clear aim and a direct outcome; and always the same effect, every time. Unfortunately, it isn't that simple. Learning is never an 'A is guaranteed to lead to B' process. And one key issue is timing. But although 'timing' is itself a simple word, it hides a complex series of ideas.

One aspect of this is duration – how long you continue with an exercise. A seemingly banal exercise, continued long past the point of boredom, can lead to a sudden breakthrough. But this is difficult to achieve in practice. Left to ourselves, few of us would stick with what feels boring and irrelevant for very long. But a good teacher, watching from the outside, can see a potential moment of breakthrough approaching and can encourage the student to persevere. He or she can also decide to prolong a particular exercise beyond the point where it 'should' finish, if it is going somewhere unexpected or useful.

If teachers are operating in a workshop situation, where time is under their individual control, it is possible to pursue duration. But for teachers working within an institutional framework of a school or university it can be more difficult. In this context teachers often have limited teaching time with the students, and may also feel under pressure to present as many exercises as possible in the time allotted. So duration can be lost.

The second key element of timing is *when* you do an exercise. This is partly a matter of a person's readiness to encounter a particular experience. One exercise encountered early in your training may have a specific effect, while the identical exercise experienced after years of training can produce radically different results. This isn't simply a case of being able to do the exercise better on a technical level; instead, the exercise actually changes its function according to skill and experience. In fact, most good acting exercises are infinite. You can do them again and again, year after year, and they will continue to yield new levels of insight and understanding. And a skilled teacher will often bring you back to the same starting point, over and over.

Because of this phenomenon, a teacher can use exactly the same exercise to explore completely different skills or concepts. For example, there is an exercise I use on physical sensitivity to space (the original source was the work of Mladen Materic). In this exercise the actors walk slowly from the back of the stage, sensing the places where the body wants to stop or change, and particularly becoming aware of the final barrier with the audience. This is usually around three or four feet away from the first row (this exercise must be done with real people in the audience – empty seats do not produce the same response). It is a very simple exercise, but it can be about physical sensitivity to one's own body reactions, or it can be about technical awareness of the 'hot' and 'cold' spots on the stage, or it can be about transgression and trespass. The exercise itself is always exactly the same, but the outcome differs each time. It all depends on how the teacher frames the exercise, which in turn depends on where the students are at that particular moment.

There is another factor involved with timing: the precise order of exercises actively changes their function and effect. Exercises are not isolated units – you don't do one, then another and a third, as if they have no relation to each other. Most teachers are aware that the exercises strung together create a specific journey through the mind and body, and a different sequence of exercises creates a different journey. If you do an exercise that is very active and energetic, followed by one that is very quiet and internal, the experience is very different from that given by the reverse order ('quiet' followed by 'energetic'). And the journey from A to B leaves you in a very different mental and emotional place from the journey from B to A.

Timing has yet another aspect: repetition. When we train, there is a danger of thinking exercises are one-off events – we do the exercise and magically the skill is transferred to us. But that isn't how real learning functions. Doing something once is simply an encounter; interesting and fun, but lacking the element of skill acquisition. We know that changing the muscle use of the body (including the voice) requires repetitive training, but many people are unaware that it also takes a number of repetitions for any new physical or emotional pattern to engrave itself on the neural circuits of the brain.

As Yoshi said, timing is the essence.

I would add another factor: subjectivity. What works for one person will be meaningless for the next. Everyone brings who they are and their history to the process, and this influences how they hear the exercises, how they apply them and what they receive as an outcome. This is why both Yoshi and I hesitate to say, 'The exercises in this book (and in our own workshops) will enable you to experience *this*, or you will learn *that*.' We cannot know what you will experience or learn.

Yoshi's workshops

Across the years, Yoshi has taught many workshops, using a huge variety of exercises derived from different sources. The exercises themselves change constantly and there is no fixed curriculum. Nevertheless, it is possible to discern certain themes that constantly recur in his teaching and the existence of a shaped journey for the student. I have outlined these below and given examples of the type of exercise he has used in various workshops in the past. Feel free to explore them, but don't be limited by these ideas. When you actually do them, you might discover something completely different. Or nothing at all.

Most workshops begin with strong physical activity, normally focused on the spine.

Exercise: Sitting undulation
Sit on the ground like a baby, with your legs in front of you. They are loosely bent, not held in any fixed position. The soles of the feet might be near each other, but you are not putting them together and then pulling them inwards. It is an easy position, with the back straight and the arms placed wherever comfortable. Then tuck the tip of the coccyx under, like a dog tucking its tail in. Keep curling the spine under, and you will find that the body moves into a backward lean. Keep the undulation going until the focus reaches the sternum. At this point, you will be leaning backwards, with the torso curved inwards, and your head tucked down and in. Your shoulders will be in front of the chest, which is caved inwards.

Then lift the sternum up and forward, using this impulse to initiate a forward movement of the torso. Focus on bringing the sternum forward and through the shoulders. The shoulders will end up behind the chest. Continue this forward movement of the sternum, and let the body follow, until you are leaning over your feet. Then tuck the tailbone under in order to initiate the undulation that moves the torso backwards. And so on; forwards and backwards. Don't try to turn it into a stretching exercise or a workout for the abdominals; keep your attention on how you initiate the two movements, tail and sternum.

Exercise: Walking undulation
This is similar to the previous exercise, except that you begin by standing. Step one foot forward, using a normal walking action. As the foot contacts the ground, let the step initiate an undulation of the spine. This begins in the pelvis, travels up through the waist, the chest, the neck and terminates with a movement of the skull. The entire spine is involved.

Then step the next foot forward and let the contact with the floor initiate a second undulation. Once you have the pattern clear (step, undulate, step, undulate and so on), you can speed up until you are walking around the space with the spine in constant movement.

As well as working on the body as a self-contained unit, Yoshi focuses on placing that body within the larger space.

Exercise: Bag of water (from The Invisible Actor)
Stand with your feet apart, the same distance as the width of your shoulders. Then try to imagine that your skin is like a plastic bag. Inside that bag there is only water – no brain, no heart, no stomach, just water, clear, crystal-clean water. Without closing your eyes you watch the water. Eventually it starts to move, to the front, to the right, to the left, to the back. It is a beautiful soft movement, just like water. At a certain moment, when you have established a clear sense of your body as water, you try to feel the earth's gravity. Some force

comes from the centre of the earth and it invites you to descend; down, down, but your flesh remains water. Your head becomes heavy, your shoulders become heavy and your arms become heavy because of the force of gravity. Gradually you sink towards the floor until you find yourself in the squatting position, with head and arms relaxed.

Then imagine that there are three threads that link your body to the sky. One of these threads connects to the top of your skull, and the other two are connected to (the back of) your wrists. The three threads start to pull you upwards into the sky, until you find yourself standing upright again, with the arms suspended in the air, as if this bag of water were hanging in the air. Then once again you feel the pull of the earth's gravity, the threads disappear, and your arms and head sink downwards, to be followed by the rest of your body (again ending in the squat position). You continue this exercise, constantly moving between the sky and earth, while the body remains water. As you repeat the movement, it gradually speeds up. Towards the end, you forget about the threads to the wrists; there is only one thread, which connects to the top of the skull. You keep going up and down for a while, without any effort, then eventually you slow down and come to a stop in the standing position. You feel as if you are suspended and balanced between the two forces of the sky and the earth.

Exercise: Symmetry
Stand in a clear space. Move any of your limbs in a completely symmetrical way. If your right arm points forwards, so does your left. If your left knee turns inwards, so does your right. Both at the same moment, not right arm first, followed by the left one. Do any kind of movement with the arms, legs, shoulders, elbows, feet and so on, even your fingers. Improvise and try to find out all the possibilities of the body while remaining completely symmetrical. If you want to move around the space you can walk (even though this isn't a symmetrical movement). But keep the rest of your body

actions symmetrical. You should also keep the head free to turn as it wants, since you need to stay aware of what is happening around you, but you can attempt to use the facial muscles symmetrically.

*   *   *

Yoshi's workshops tend to follow a clear progression; the exercises begin with the body of the individual actor (see above), then he moves into areas of greater complexity. After the initial work on the body, he often introduces one of his key ideas: a focus on *how* you do the exercise, emphasising the need for attentiveness to process, both internal (within the actor) and external (around the actor).

One key concept is *tasting*. (This idea is mentioned in Chapter 2, where Yoshi talks about the importance of 'tasting' as a means to ensure that bridges and transitions are organic rather than artificially constructed.) To taste an action you bring your awareness into your body and sense the quality of that action as it is happening. As you move from A to B, you sense what the next moment needs; what feels appropriate. The emphasis in 'tasting' is on 'feeling at this exact moment', not 'planning in advance'.

Exercise: Tasting
Choose four different hand positions, using one hand only. Maybe position A is the fist clenched tightly, facing downwards. Position B could be a relaxed hand facing upwards, while C might be a flattened hand facing inwards with the fingers held closely together and D is any other position. The exact positions don't matter; you can choose what you like. You start with the first hand position (A) and sense how the hand can transform itself into position B. Then you taste position B, and sense how the tranformation occurs to position C. And so on to D.

It is important to feel that it is not 'you', but the hand itself making the shift. If you don't do this, but instead only watch your hand from the outside, it becomes mechanical. Tasting is essential.

Transformation is not via looking at the hand and deciding, 'Oh, that would be a good way to transform.'

* * *

As well as promoting sensitivity to inner process, Yoshi's work also emphasises alertness to external events.

Exercise

With a large group of actors you make a square with approximately even numbers along each side. For example, if you have sixteen people, you make a square with four sides of four. There are four sides – side A, side B, side C and side D – going consecutively round the square. You start on side A. One person walks across the square in six beats (keeping in time with the beat) and joins the people on side C. The next side to act is side B, where two people walk across the square to join the people on side D. The next side (side C) sends three people across the square to join side A. On side D four people walk across. Then back to side A where five people walk across. Then we start again with one person travelling across the square from side B, then two from side C and so on: four sides and from one to five people travelling across. You travel round the square from A to B to C to D to A and so on. And the numbers move consecutively from one to five round the square. This is all done on a steady beat and the people who are walking across 'choose' themselves. If the count is for five people and there are five people on that side, all of them travel across. But if the count is for two people and three people start across, someone has to realise that they are not needed and run back to their originating side of the square. If the count is for five people and there are only two actors on that side at that time both walk across, although everybody has to remember that the two people they see walking actually represent a group of five and that the next number will be one not three. Because the population on the various sides keeps changing, the actors have to stay very alert to where they are in the space sequence and the time sequence.

Once this pattern has been established, you make it more complex by changing the time sequence. Instead of starting each round at one, reverse the order. You count as far as five, then the next number is four, followed by three, followed by two and back to one, which is then followed by two, then three.

* * *

Usually the next stage of Yoshi's workshops involve greater complexity, such as responding to other actors, or the use of objects. And central to this complexity is the idea of change. Yoshi says that the actor's job is to reproduce human life. Not like a documentary, but via an awareness of its essential nature, which according to him is a process of constant change. Therefore if actors want to stay true to life, they must be aware of the need to change – constantly – and be able to do this organically.

To begin this process Yoshi often introduces improvisations using objects. The emphasis is on full exploration without commentary or attempts at characterisation. In other words to discover the possibilities of simple actions, rather than decorating or overtly performing these actions in order to make them more interesting. The main factors to play with in this area are as follows: body (changes of tempo and shape), speech (changes of tempo, pitch and volume).

Exercise: Objects

Get a table, a chair, a teapot, teacup, spoon and saucer. Place the objects on the table. The basic pattern is: walk in, sit down, pour a cup of tea (you don't need real water, just mime the action) and drink it. Within this framework, explore the various possibilities, using changes of tempo, pauses, shifts of weight and so on. For example, you might lift the teapot, pause for several seconds, then slowly bring the pot towards the cup.

Keep the actions natural and realistic, rather than creative or stylised in any way. Work with the key variations outlined above.

Also, play with the weight of the body; what happens when you drink the tea with your weight forward rather than back, when sitting in the chair. And as you explore the hundreds of possibilities, taste each one to see how it feels.

* * *

As the workshop progresses, more and more complexity is introduced, including responding to other actors, the use of language and multi-layered work (such as the integration of object work with responding to other actors).

Exercise (from The Invisible Actor*)*
Two people sit on the floor and exchange a conversation with each other, using only the actions of one hand. Person A makes a gesture towards person B, who then replies to A with another gesture. To which A replies and so on. Like a conversation, the communication passes back and forth between the two actors. This must be a communication of direct impulses, not social gestures (like shaking hands), or charades (where gestures replace words, as in crooking the finger and beckoning to represent 'come here').

Try to concentrate your whole existence into that one hand. It is a kind of strange animal. When you find the genuine life of this creature, and it is able to develop a real and varied relationship with the other animal, it is fascinating to watch . . . What is interesting is the exchange. The 'acting' doesn't reside in the hand of each actor; it exists in the air between the two hands. This kind of acting is not narrative, not psychology, not emotion, but something else, something more basic.

Exercise
This has the same starting point as the previous object exercise, except that there are two chairs instead of one. You work with a partner, but retain only one teapot, teacup and saucer. Person A makes the first action, while B watches. Then B responds, while A

watches. For example, A sits down in the chair, then B reaches for the teapot. Person A then responds by reaching for the cup and so on. Again the key is to avoid demonstrating or enacting intellectual choices. The goal is simple direct response between two human beings.

* * *

The same kind of direct responding can be done with the element of speech.

Exercise: Yes/No

Two actors sit on the floor facing each other. Actor A has the word 'Yes' and actor B the word 'No'. Actor A says 'Yes' to actor B, with a clear tone and intention. The word 'Yes' can be said in a cautionary whisper, or as a sharp assertion, or with a teasing smile. Or even as a seductive question. Actor B replies with the word 'No', but must follow the same intention posited by actor A. So if actor A says 'Yes' as a tease, then B must continue to tease, but using the word 'No'. Actor A then becomes more insistent with the teasing and says once again 'Yes' in reply to the 'No'. And B becomes even more provocative when answering for the second time. The aim is to keep building the action *without* changing the tactic (in this case 'teasing'). It is very easy for the 'No' person simply to refuse the game by saying 'No' in an angry tone, or for A to change tactic when the first strategy (in this case 'teasing') fails to work (i.e. make person A agree and say 'Yes' instead of 'No'). The two actors continue to exchange their two words, while allowing the tactic to grow and become increasingly intense, until the game reaches its natural end point when both actors sense the climax has been reached and the 'scene' has ended itself organically. This is sensed, not planned, and usually the natural end point is much further along than would be socially comfortable in daily life.

In this exercise the characters are in direct conflict (one says 'Yes' and the other totally disagrees, using the word 'No'). But as actors, the two individuals are in total agreement and harmony. Together they build the scene and take the chosen tactic as far as it can possibly go. In addition, a sense of theatrical timing emerges; the actors sense how long they must continue to develop their conversation in order to reach the natural end point or climax. The key technique is to *develop* the conversation one step further with each exchange; if actor B simply echoes the tactic offered by A, the action cannot move onwards. And it cannot end organically; it will simply fizzle out through boredom.

* * *

Yoshi tends to use four basic breath patterns: breathe in, stop the breath at the top of the in-breath, breathe out, stop the breath at the bottom of the out-breath. He also suggests that the students be aware of ('taste') how each of them feels.

Exercise
Stand facing your partner, who is standing on the opposite side of the room. At first, quite naturally, breathe in and breathe out. Then, without thinking about your breath, look at your partner and say 'hello'. Repeat the same action but deliberately change the breathing pattern. This time, breathe in consciously and say 'hello'. See how that feels. Then try a third pattern: breathe out (while retaining a little air in the lungs) and say 'hello'. See if there is a difference. Try a fourth alternative: breathe out first, then snatch a quick breath in and say 'hello'. What you feel and what your partner receives may be different each time.

In the next stage combine breath with movement. Breathe in, block the breath at the top, walk normally towards your partner, arrive in front of him or her and say 'hello'. Then try another version: breathe out, stop the breath, walk to your partner and say 'hello'.

You can also play with the speed at which you breathe in and out. For example, before you say the word 'hello', breathe in quickly and see how that feels. Then do it again, slowly.

You can apply this approach, too, when speaking text. If there is a pause between two phrases, don't take a breath immediately after finishing the first line. Wait with almost empty lungs, then take a quick in-breath just before you speak the next line. Or the other way round: finish your text, breathe in, hold the in-breath during the pause, then speak. See how it feels to do it in different ways. Normally, actors just slowly breathe in during the pause and go on to the next line. But it is interesting to play around with the different breath possibilities.

* * *

This gives a little the flavour of a workshop with Yoshi. If you explore these exercises, remember that the impact of what you do will depend on the precise timing. And the timing itself depends on the insight of the teacher, as well as on the institutional structuring of time. Yoshi teaches in week-long workshops (minimum), which last six hours a day. He therefore has the freedom to shape the student's journey and to use time in the most beneficial way. This degree of freedom is not the norm in most institution-based training.

In addition, Yoshi is very aware of the diagnostic role of the teacher. It isn't enough to set up an exercise and simply let it run its course. For advanced work, the student needs detailed feedback about where and when the exercise goes wrong. When you work with Yoshi, he tells you exactly when you start demonstrating or performing in an inorganic way, usually at the moment you do it. It can be daunting to receive, but it is necessary. However, this kind of critique can be counter-productive unless undertaken by an experienced teacher working with students who are already fully committed to their own journey.

Good Luck!